RUBBER TOY VEHICLES

IDENTIFICATION & VALUE GUIDE

DAVE LEOPARD

COLLECTOR BOOKS

A Division of Schroeder Publishing Co., Inc.

Front cover: Clockwise from top right: Curtiss P-37 Pursuit plane (Auburn), Open Racer (Sun), 1936 Teardrop sedan (Sun), John Deere "A" farm tractor (Auburn), 1947 Chevrolet truck (Auburn), Open Racer (Auburn), 1940 Oldsmobile sedan (Auburn), 1935 Oldsmobile coupe (Rainbow). Back, top: Pursuit ship (Sun), bottom: 1940 Dodge sedan (Sun).

Cover design by Beth Summers
Book design by Kelly Dowdy

COLLECTOR BOOKS
P.O. Box 3009
Paducah, Kentucky 42002-3009
www.collectorbooks.com

Copyright © 2003 David M. Leopard

David M. Leopard
2507 Feather Run Trail
West Columbia, SC 29169-4915

The current values in this book should be used only as a guide. They are not intended to set prices, which vary from one section of the country to another. Auction prices as well as dealer prices vary greatly and are affected by condition as well as demand. Neither the author nor the publisher assumes responsibility for any losses that might be incurred as a result of consulting this guide.

Searching For A Publisher?

We are always looking for people knowledgeable within their fields. If you feel that there is a real need for a book on your collectible subject and have a large comprehensive collection, contact Collector Books.

CONTENTS

DEDICATION

This book is dedicated to all the rubber toy collectors, who appreciate the beauty of these small toys that were only around for about 20 years. They made a great impact on many of us as we were growing up, and today we enjoy them more than ever.

ACKNOWLEDGMENTS

To re-publish a book is a risky endeavor, unless the new book is significantly better than the original. My personal collection has grown, as well as my knowledge of rubber toys, but what really makes this book so much better than the original is the great input I have received from other collectors. Since the original publication, I have received a steady flow of feedback, photos, and priceless tidbits of information that have enabled me to take the book to a new level.

Nelson Adams, Steve Butler, Berni Carlson, Dennis Dawson, Larry Forte, Steve Kelley, Carl Natter, Pim Piet, and Gates Willard have provided photographs, without which the book would fall far short in the coverage of rare vehicles. Likewise, Dennis Dawson, Richard O'Brien, and Howard Steinberg have shared the wonderful old catalogs that add so much to the substance of these pages.

A special thanks to Charley Maledon, who, over the years, has always kept in touch and shared every new find with me.

Thanks to Tom Bishop, who took our knowledge of Glolite toys to new heights and shared these great catalog pages with us.

Charlie Sapp's contributions are truly significant and help us relate toy history to automobile history.

I met Dick Ford through the Antique Toy Collectors of America and he has shared his wealth of knowledge, along with many photos that provide a new insight into the use of rubber toys as promotionals.

Hope McCandlish Rider is the daughter of Edward McCandlish, who worked for Auburn Rubber during the early years. He was an artist and designer and was instrumental in Auburn's growth and success in the toy field. Hope provided a rare catalog page and wonderful insight into the Auburn history.

Many of the high-quality photographs of rare and unusual toys were provided by Ron Snow and Bill Ferretti. I met Bill and Ron through the Internet and they bring new meaning to the term "serious collector." Their contributions have gone above and beyond anything I could have hoped for. Bill has contributed the entire section on Duravits and is the leading authority on these Argentinian toys.

Thanks to Jack Owen, a Columbia photographer who does beautiful wedding portraits, and beautiful toy portraits, as well.

A very special thanks to John West, whom I have known and admired for many years. John allowed me to print his famous Sun Rubber Company drawing, which originally appeared in the November 1997 issue of *Antique Toy World*. John has also very graciously provided a foreword to this book, which I truly treasure.

FOREWORD

Collecting antique rubber toys is easy. All the collector has to do is find them and arrange them on a shelf... because Dave Leopard has done all the leg-work, fact-finding, letter-writing and phone-calling to locate the research he has put together in this book.

I collect rubber cars and trucks because they are handsome miniatures of some of my favorite marques of the 1930s and 1940s. They have an accuracy and detail that is not present in automobile toys made of other materials.

If the collector has any questions, or wishes to identify a certain antique rubber toy... all he has to do is read this book because Dave Leopard knows more about the rubber vehicles of our childhood than any other person on the face of the earth!

—John West - Nov. 2002

PREFACE

HISTORY OF RUBBER TOYS

Rubber toy vehicles seemed to suddenly appear on the scene in 1935, and almost as suddenly disappeared in 1955. Let's examine the circumstances under which they came and departed.

In 1935, the U.S. economy was improving from the depths of the Great Depression, but many families continued to struggle just to pay for the basic necessities of life. The toy industry, like U.S. industries in general, was becoming more and more cost conscious. They needed to find a way to cut costs in basic materials, labor, and distribution, particularly shipping.

The American rubber manufacturing industry was well established in metropolitan centers like Akron and Pittsburgh. They had skilled labor that could easily be adapted to the production of toys. Natural raw rubber was readily available, shipped from the South Pacific through the port of Singapore, and on to the rubber manufacturing centers by rail.

Auburn, Sun, and other rubber companies had already established that rubber was a very workable and attractive material for the production of dolls, soldiers, and other animal and human figures. To make rubber toy vehicles was a very natural and logical step.

Toy vehicles had been around since real vehicles had been around. Horse-drawn, and later motorized vehicles were made of tin, cast iron, and lead since the nineteenth century. The mid-thirties brought a great interest in automobiles across the country. The automotive industry was perhaps in its most flamboyant stage, with many beautiful luxury cars on the market. It was also about the time that "affordable" cars like Fords became more attractive and sporty. Toy automobiles became very popular during this era and rubber cars were the mainstay of the low-priced field.

The late thirties and early forties saw rubber toy manufacturers flourish and prosper. Several companies shared the market and many new toys were introduced up through 1941. All toy production was shut down during World War II and most rubber companies shifted their capacity to war production. After the war, both Auburn and Sun continued production of some of their pre-war models and added a few toys to their line.

By the mid-fifties, rubber toys were squeezed out of the market by competition from plastic toys. Rising costs in rubber production (particularly union labor) simply did not allow rubber toys to be manufactured and marketed at a price that could compete with American-made plastic toys. The last new rubber toy was introduced by Auburn in 1953, and the last year any rubber toy was included in a catalog was 1956.

THE DIME STORE

Some people called them five and dimes. Others called them ten cent stores. Perhaps really proper people called them variety stores. Where I grew up they were always called dime stores.

When Frank Winfield Woolworth opened his first store in Utica, New York, it was called the Great 5-Cent Store. That store quickly failed and he re-opened in Lancaster, Pennsylvania, in 1879. It was a big success and this great American institution was born. Hot on Woolworth's heels, John Graham McCrorey opened his first store in Scottdale, Pennsylvania. In 1883, both stores added 10-cent items to their stock. It was not until 1932 that Woolworth raised its top price to 20 cents. By 1935 none of America's established chains had a price limit.

By the thirties, hundreds of stores across the nation bore the familiar gold letters on the red background. Woolworth, McCrorey, Kress, Kresge, Silver's, Green's, Newberry's, McLellan's, Grant's, and Murphy's were all names kids recognized and cherished. Depending on which part of the country you lived in and the size of your town, you probably had one or more of these fabulous emporiums available to you.

My memories of visiting the dime store as a small child are as clear as a bell. The sights, the sounds, and the smells are at instant recall. The stores were impressive structures with ceilings made from embossed tin with fancy designs. The doors were often swinging doors made of brass. The floors were made from heavy hardwood planking — maple mostly, but some were made from walnut and other expensive woods. The floors were regularly oiled and were swept clean every day with huge push brooms.

Your nose could lead you to the distinctive smell of oil cloth, which was displayed at the rear of the store on large rolls, ready to be cut to fit your kitchen table. The smell I remember most vividly is that of the hot roasted nuts in huge glass containers, kept warm by lamps and waiting to be scooped up into little bags that quickly began soaking up the oil from these delicious treats. Of course, the nuts were accompanied by countless varieties of candy — always fresh and tempting. I remember the solid milk chocolate candy that was prepared in thick sheets and broken up into chunks for serving to the customer.

Keith Marvin, who grew up around Albany and Troy, New York, during the thirties, remembers the music counter, where you could buy phonograph records for about 25 cents each and you could try them out to see if you liked them. The big recording companies, like Columbia and Victor, did not sell their top-line records in dime stores but offered companion brands, like Harmony, Velvet Tone, or Bluebird for the 25 cent market. Keith also fondly recalls that you could buy sheet music for 10 cents each and you could ask the store pianist to play it for you.

Bing Crosby recorded a big hit called "Million Dollar Baby." He found her selling china in a five and ten cent store, where he went to escape a sudden summer shower. Of course, the story ended as all good love stories ended during that innocent era — they got married and lived happily ever after!

My mother would take me to the dime store and let me linger around the toy counters while she shopped for patterns, fabric, or other sewing needs. I would quickly speed past the "girl's" section, with all its colorful array of lithographed tea sets and paper dolls, and zero in on the "good stuff."

I had more than a passing interest in cap pistols and lead soldiers but my real love was the cars and trucks that were neatly arranged between thick glass dividers. My heart would pound, I'm sure, because I would probably be allowed to pick one thing to buy and that would have to be something inexpensive. But the choices were so hard! Those colorful little Tootsietoys. A sturdy Wyandotte truck. Charming little Barclay toys. In the end, often times the choice would come down to one rubber car or another. Perhaps it was the smell. I loved to pick up those shiny new rubber toys and smell them. In any case, my love affair with rubber toys began long ago, and is still going strong!

The dime stores are almost gone now. The Kreske chain turned into K-Mart. Sam Walton, who started with Ben Franklin stores, created the Wal-Mart empire. Big cities still have dime stores but many of those are turning up in shopping malls, as downtown shopping areas continue to erode. There are still plenty of places for today's kids to buy toy cars, but they are all sealed in plastic. They will never know the joy of sniffing a fresh rubber Oldsmobile in the dime store.

INTRODUCTION

One of the most critical, and most difficult steps for a writer is to "define the universe." In other words, determine what will be included in the book and, as a direct result, determine what will not be included.

As a toy collector, I am interested in toy cars and trucks of all types, but essentially limit my collection to:

1. American made (including Canadian)

2. Small scale, mostly 12 inches or less in length

3. Made during the period 1920 – 1960

My favorite sub-set of this broad collecting interest is rubber toys and that was a natural selection for my subject. That is still a pretty big universe and one of my objectives in writing this book was to limit the scope to the point that it would be complete and an undisputed source of information for collectors. I limited the scope in three ways: 1) type of toy, 2) type of material used, and 3) period of time during which the toys were manufactured.

My first attempt at defining the type of toy was very narrow. We would include cars and trucks and related special-purpose vehicles like fire engines and racers — nothing else. As my research began to take shape, I realized that there were so few of the other motorized vehicles (trains, aircraft, farm tractors, etc.) that they should be included as well. Another logical step was to include farm implements that were pulled by the tractors. We consciously drew the line at motorized forms of transportation and things that would have been pulled by them (trailers for example). One could make an excellent case for including farm wagons pulled by horses, but then you might be tempted to include all horses and farm animals, and there goes your nice, neat boundary!

The type of material the toys were made of is rubber, pure and simple. It can be natural or synthetic. The toy may be solid, molded, or hollow but it must be rubber. There is a strong case for including vinyl because the Auburn Rubber Company switched over from rubber to vinyl and continued making toys for another 15 years. This book is not about the Auburn Rubber Company, however, even though they contributed greatly, but it is about rubber toys in general and the unique role they played in American toy history.

The period of time we elected to cover was the easiest of the three variables to pin down. The beginning is easy. As best we can tell, the first rubber toy vehicle was produced in 1934 and the industry thrived through 1942, when toy production was shut down because of the war. Many of the companies that made rubber toys during the thirties, never returned to toy production after the war. Auburn and Sun both returned to toy production in 1946 with their old, pre-war models. Both companies actually introduced a few new rubber toys during the post-war period. The last new toys introduced by Sun were rolled out in 1947. From that point on, they were in a state of decline, as far as rubber vehicles were concerned. Auburn brought out some new models as late as 1953. These models were short-lived, however, since all Auburn rubber vehicles were phased out in favor of vinyl by 1956. The life of rubber toy vehicles in the United States is actually less than 20 years, 1934 – 1953, with three years out during World War II.

I would have stopped right there but I chose to include a piece about Unique Toys, manufactured during the 1970s – 1980s, because they represent the only serious attempt in the United States to return to rubber toy production since the fifties. I have also included a small sampling of more recent rubber toys made in foreign countries, to illustrate that there were still small pockets of interest in rubber toys in other countries into the seventies.

9

MODEL DIFFERENCES

If one is to catalog toys with an intent to determine how many different "models" were made, how do you decide what constitutes a difference? This is a philosophical issue, and collectors vary greatly in their opinions. I can only describe my own philosophy, with the full understanding that many collectors will disagree.

First, let us list all the ways a model can be different:

1. Obvious difference in make and model, e.g., a 1935 Ford or a 1937 Oldsmobile.

2. Size. Some models were identical, except for size. Toy manufacturers always liked to have a toy to fill every price range, and size was a major determinant of cost and price. Auburn Metro cabover trucks provide a good example.

3. Accessories. Some models were made into specialized versions by adding some accessory to give it a different appearance. For example, adding a canvas cover with a red cross on it, changed an Auburn truck into an ambulance.

4. Mold differences — external. Sometimes, manufacturers created new molds with differences. These differences could be slight, perhaps even accidental, or they could be intentional, designed to make the toy better or perhaps less expensive to produce. A good example of slight differences is found in Auburn 1937 Oldsmobiles and 1939 Plymouths. Some have features like windshield wipers, door handles, or trunk handles, and others don't. These are differences that require close scrutiny. A more obvious change is found in the Auburn Lincoln convertible. It was done in two versions, one of which has significantly more detail and major differences in appearance, e.g., shape of the headlights.

5. Mold differences — internal. These are differences that are not readily apparent when looking at the toy until you turn it over. These differences may be grouped into three sub-sets:
   a. Changes to the way wheels or axles are mounted.
   b. Changes to the under-structure, usually designed to make the toy sturdier or less likely to warp.
   c. Changes to printing or trademarks. For example, some Auburn toys are marked with the "ARCOR" trademark, others, identical in every other way, are marked "Auburn," or "AUB-RUBR."

6. Changes in tires or axles. Over time, most rubber toys were switched from white tires to black tires and axle styles were also changed.

7. Colors. Toys may be painted in different colors to provide variety and choice, but they may also be painted in such a way as to make the vehicle appear very different. Conversion of a sedan to a taxi or a panel truck to an amblance is simply a matter of paint, with the added trim or decals to complete the image. There is no difference in the mold, however.

For the purpose of identifying different models in this book, I use the first three categories (model, size, accessories) and sometimes the fourth category — mold differences — if the differences are obvious. I chose not to include internal mold differences, even though you can make a good case that you should distinguish between them as different models. I did not, because it would greatly increase the number of "models" cataloged, but the differences would not be visable from a photograph. The last two categories, tires/axles, and colors, are easily disposed of because there is no way to insure that the toy in your hand is as it left the factory. Paint and tires are easily changed over the years.

This photo provides a good example of internal mold differences. Both are AR04. The early version at the top had a weakness that caused the axles to tear out of the holes. The re-designed version, which corrected that problem, has more support cross-pieces, which also results in less warping.

NUMBERING SYSTEM

We devised this numbering system so that collectors could have a standard point of reference when describing rubber toy vehicles. It is a simple system that uses a four-position alpha-numeric code to define a particular toy.

The first position (alpha) represents the toy manufacturer, distributor, or brand name. If known, manufacturer is the preferred descriptor. In some cases, e.g., Giftcraft, we are sure who distributed the toy but cannot say for certain who actually manufactured it. In the case of Toyco, we do not know who manufactured or distributed the toy, but it bears the name "Toyco" on the decal. When we cannot identify a toy by any of these means, we have no choice but to label it "unknown."

A = Auburn	P = Perfect	D = Duravit	S = Sun	J = Judy	R = Rainbow
T = Giftcraft	B = Barr	E = Glolite	F = Firestone	V = Viceroy	G = Seiberling
U = Unknown	C = Toyco	M = Empire			

The second position (alpha) represents the vehicle type, in broad terms:

A = Auto/Station Wagon	F = Farm Tractor/Construction	T = Truck/Bus/Ambulance
N = Train	I = Farm Tractor Implements	B = Boat/Ship/Submarine
E = Fire Engine	C = Motorcycle	R = Racer
D = Disney Toy (all types)	M = Military	P = Aircraft (plane)

The third and fourth positions (numerical) are serially assigned in logical groupings. They are not necessarily in the order in which they were manufactured or marketed but are grouped by prototype as much as possible. For example, all Auburn Oldsmobiles are grouped together, regardless of their chronological order in the product line.

Since *Rubber Toy Vehicles* was originally published, several new varieties have been discovered. Where these are not signigicant enough to warrant a new designation, we are assigned an "A" after the code. For example see Auburn AA02 and AA02A.

This numbering system is completely flexible, in that new varieties may be easily added without disrupting the previously established codes. Toys that are currently categorized as "unknown" will, hopefully, be identified in the future, at which time they will be assigned a permanent code and dropped from the unknown list.

PRICES

I have included a price as a broad reference for collectors. The value range is assigned to toys in excellent to near mint condition. Boxes would increase the value listed.

The value of rubber toy vehicles has increased significantly over the past several years and even as we go to press there is no end in sight to this trend. The value for the more common varieties is somewhat stable — not much increase since this guide was first published. Prices have soared, however, for the high-end rubber toys — those that are rare or in mint condition.

During the past twenty years, I have examined thousands of rubber toys and have bought and sold hundreds. The value I place on these toys is essentially what I think they are worth to me — in other words, what I would be willing to pay if I did not own the toy. I assume no responsibility for the validity of these values in a specific market at a specific time.

Toys that are marked "rare" exist in such small numbers that it is impossible to assign a value to them. In most cases, these are toys I have not seen offered for sale.

THE AUBURN RUBBER COMPANY

William H. Willennar and A. L. Murray of Auburn, Indiana, formed the Double Fabric Tire Company in 1910 and located their plant on East Seventh Street in their hometown. The company made inner soles and tire patches and later expanded their line to include automobile tires and tubes. The business was quickly successful and by 1912 they employed 62 workers and found they had outgrown their facility. They expanded into the McIntyre Building on West Ninth Street in Auburn and relocated most of their equipment to the new site.

The young company was shaken by disaster in 1913 when a raging fire destroyed the entire city block that surrounded the McIntyre Building. The Double Fabric Tire Company lost essentially all of its machinery, equipment, and raw materials. There were strong rumors that the firm would fold but they were well insured and were able to rebuild. They constructed a new plant of 184,000 square feet in West Auburn and were soon back in business. During the twenties, the company was reorganized as the Auburn Rubber Company. Mr. Willennar retired in 1924, selling his interest to his partner, Mr. Murray. The Auburn Rubber Company continued to grow during the twenties and was considered to be one of the most financially secure companies in the United States.

Dave Sellew, A. L. Murray's nephew, served as vice president and in 1935 was named president and general manager of the company. Despite the stereotype image of the "boss's nephew" we have all seen bear the brunt of many jokes, Sellew was, by all accounts, a very capable and well liked manager that would serve Auburn commendably for many years. Dave Sellew was no doubt a key figure in the decision to redirect Auburn's main business to toy production during the thirties – fifties.

GOD SPEED, TODAY!

Ride 'em up hill
And ride 'em down,
Ride 'em all
Around the town.

Tell 'em Sonny
Has a birthday –
Two years old!
God speed, today!"

The Lord be with you.

In 1935, A. L. Murray travelled to Europe and returned with a number of souvenirs, including a palace guard lead soldier. Murray thought the soldier could be molded from rubber and would sell in the toy market. He hired a local pattern maker to make a mold and produced a batch of the rubber palace guards. Murray arranged for local free-lance artist Edward McCandlish to hand decorate the soldiers. After one showing to some toy buyers, the orders poured in and Auburn found itself in the toy business. They soon added baseball and football figures to the line that would continue to grow for the next twenty years.

Auburn produced its first rubber toy vehicle in 1936 — a beautiful Cord sedan, done with great attention to detail. Their second vehicle, a 1935 Ford, reflects the same fine detail as did all the others that followed until World War II put a halt to toy production. The local availability of many talented automotive designers and pattern makers was no doubt a factor in Auburn's decision to manufacture toy automobiles that looked real. Auburn, Indiana, with its tradition of fine automobiles, like the Cord, Auburn, and Duesenberg, was a perfect breeding ground for new ideas in toy production.

Between 1936 and 1942, the Auburn Rubber Company continued to expand its line of rubber vehicles to include trucks, tractors, airplanes, ships, motorcycles, and fire engines. Rubber figures, including many varieties of soldiers and athletes continued to grow as well and the company held a substantial position in the toy industry when the war began.

During World War II, Auburn turned its resources to the production of goods to support the defense effort. They produced rubber soles, gaskets, and other items needed to fight the war but never completely lost interest in toy production. The company experimented with making toys from various non-strategic materials, such as sawdust, but nothing really proved successful.

When the war was over, Auburn was overwhelmed with demand for toys, but could not immediately wind down production of the other products. As a stop-gap measure, they bought a plant in Connellsville, Pennsylvania, and tooled up to produce toys again. During the late forties, all of the Auburn toys were produced in Pennsylvania, while the Auburn, Indiana, plant continued the non-toy lines. In 1950, they added capacity at the old Auburn site and resumed toy production there.

In 1952, Auburn got into the plastic injection molding business and made the decision to phase out rubber toys in favor of vinyl. The new rubber-like vinyl toys were first introduced in the 1953 catalog and by 1955 almost all rubber toys had been replaced by vinyl equivalents. The 1956 catalog included none of the old rubber line.

In 1960, the toy products division of Auburn was purchased by the city of Deming, New Mexico. Deming desperately needed new industry and could offer

Hydraulic presses are of the multiple platen type and the molds are either pressed aluminum or die cut steel to insure sharpness of detail.

Freight cars approach the Auburn plant on the company's spur. Trucks are loaded at the shipping department exits. Four railroads intersect in Auburn, two trans-continental east-west federal highways are a few miles away and two main line north-south roads pass through the city

low-cost labor. The move cost 200 employees their jobs in Auburn, Indiana, but the loss was somewhat offset by Cooper Tire and Rubber Company, who purchased the old Auburn plant and continues to use it. The Deming operation lasted only a few years and the company filed for bankruptcy in 1969.

AUBURN RUBBER CORPORATION
AUBURN INDIANA
1939

ORGANIZED 1910
EMPLOYS 400-550

Raw rubber from Singapore is masticated in the three Banbury Mixers, from formulas worked out by the Laboratory. In these machines, the necessary ingredients are thoroughly dispersed with the rubber.

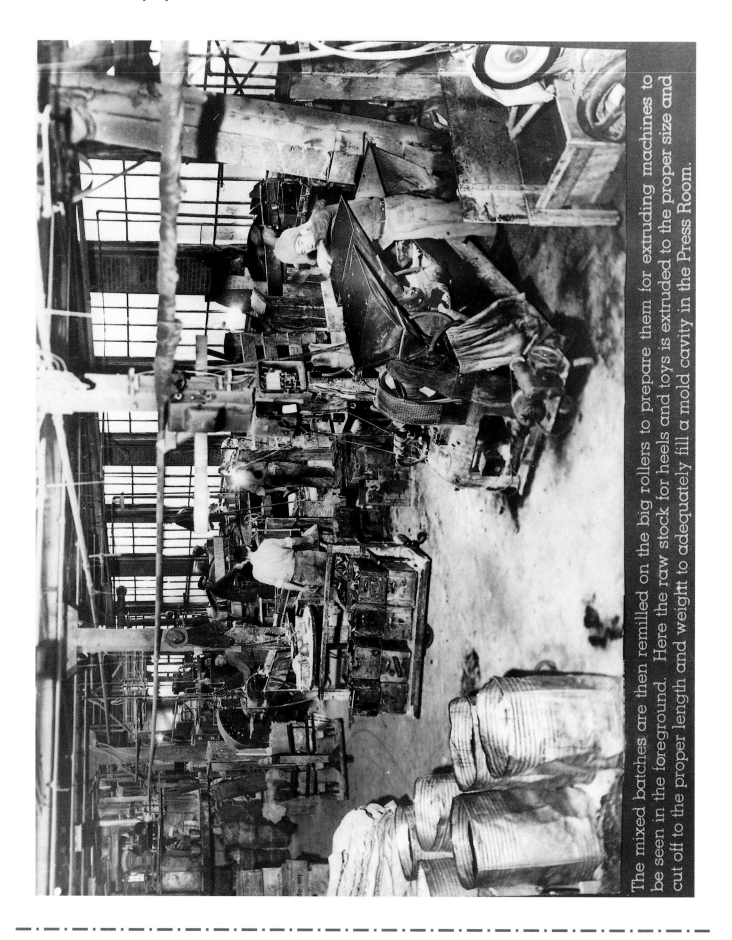

The mixed batches are then remilled on the big rollers to prepare them for extruding machines to be seen in the foreground. Here the raw stock for heels and toys is extruded to the proper size and cut off to the proper length and weight to adequately fill a mold cavity in the Press Room.

The rubber is placed in molds under two-thousand pounds of hydraulic pressure and vulcanized in the shape of the mold by live steam. Presses run 24 hours daily producing uniform heat and

Toys must have the bleed or overflow of rubber removed. Depending on the type of item, they are either tumbled, buffed or die-trimmed.

On this conveyor the assembling is continuous including dipping, assembly of wheels and axles, hand decorating, and, in the near foreground, inspection and sorting.

From the time the toys are dipped until they go down the chute in the foreground to the Shipping Room, the operation is continuous. In the background the toys are coming off of the decorating conveyors and are being inspected before being packed into containers and then into shipping cartons. Boxed sets are assembled from bins of bulk toys, just as they come from this packing conveyor.

Auburn, Indiana:-Beautiful, Progressive, Hospitable

Auburn Country Club

Y. M. C. A.

Home of the Auburn Commercial Club—(left)
City Hall—(right)

Hotel Auburn

City National Bank (left) — Court House Square — Auburn State Bank (right)

Eckhart Public Library

Court House (left) — Masonic Home (right)

Plant of the Auburn Rubber Co.

Eckhart Park

AUBURN

"Loveliest Village of the Plain," the county seat of DeKalb County, is situated in the fertile St. Joe River Valley on the southern border of the beautiful lake region of Northeastern Indiana.

It is about equi-distant from Chicago, Detroit, Cleveland, Columbus and Indianapolis, with a population of over 7,000,000 within the Second Parcel Post Zone.

This commercially strategic location, excellent shipping facilities over the Baltimore & Ohio, New York Central, Pennsylvania and Interurban railroads, abundant electric power at reasonable rates, and the splendid labor conditions which have always prevailed in this community, make Auburn a prosperous manufacturing city.

Auburn is widely known as the home of the Auburn Automobile and the Auburn Tire.

Some of its other numerous industries are: Gladiator Manufacturing Co., The Auburn Post Card Mfg. Co., The Auburn Printing Co., The Auburn Foundry, The Auburn Metal Products Co., The Reike Metal Products Co., DeKalb Furniture Mfg. Co., Auburn Novelty Works, Globe Superior Garment Co., Sterlite Foundry and Mfg. Co., Frank E. Davis Fish Co.

The prosperity of Auburn is not alone due to its manufacturing plants, but also to the rich farming country surrounding it. There are two reliable banks with combined assets of over $2,500,000, and a Post Office of the first class, with eleven incoming and fourteen outgoing mails daily.

Auburn is noted for its splendid public buildings. The Auburn Commercial Club owns its $50,000 home and enjoys the unique distinction of having 300 active farmer members out of a total membership of 600. The large and well equipped Y. M. C. A. and the beautiful Public Library were gifts of public spirited citizens.

Auburn has exceptionally good schools, many churches and up-to-date stores, a fine golf course and country club open all the year, a beautiful city park, two theaters, ten miles of paved streets, fine homes and a harmonious all-American population.

The clean, moral atmosphere, wholesome surroundings and healthful living conditions make Auburn an ideal city in which to live.

McIntosh High School

Auburn 8-88 Sedan

For further information write the Secretary of the Auburn Commercial Club

TRADEMARKS

Auburn was a very aggressive company that never ceased looking for a new gimmick — a new advertising twist, a new way to display or promote the toys, or a new trademark. Looking back over the way they marked and promoted their toys makes one wonder why they didn't simply leave well enough alone!

Their vast array of trademarks has been a source of confusion for toy collectors for many years. Of course, Auburn was trying to sell toys at the time and had no idea these inexpensive rubber playthings would become prized collectibles!

Between the time Auburn rolled their first car off the assembly line in 1936 and about 1953, when rubber toys were almost gone from the scene, they used five principal ways to mark their toys. They also used at least six more trademarks in their literature that didn't actually appear on the toys. In addition, they occasionally used multiple trademarks on a single toy. If that was not confusing enough, on more than one occasion, they seemed to abandon use of a particular trademark or way they marked toys for a year or more, only to resume using it.

Having said all that, the reader must understand that tracking an Auburn toy or literature over time, based on how it is marked, is very tricky business. Following is a rough guide to how/when toys are marked:

1. From 1936 until 1942, when toy production was shut down for the war, Auburn used the following underneath most toys.

AUBURN RUBBER CORP.
AUBURN, IND.

Toys that were actually manufactured during the early post-war years from the old pre-war molds were marked the same way.

2. From 1937 until 1942, and again after the war through 1948, Auburn used this marking:

AUB-RUBR Auburn, Ind.
Made in U.S.A.

3. For a short time, perhaps 1948 – 1951, they adopted this trademark:

ARCOR SAFE PLAY TOYS

4. For an even shorter time, 1952 – 1953, they used this version:

AUBURN TRADE MARK REG Auburn, Ind.

5. The last few rubber toys manufactured before they switched to vinyl, bore no trademark or imprint of any kind underneath the toy except for a small mold number. These toys had external markings that told the buyer they were Auburn toys. For example, the firetruck bore the markings "Auburn F.D." on the hood and the large truck (AT10) simply bore the "Auburn" marking across the side of the bed. This practice continued into the vinyl line of toys, at least for a while.

In addition to these imprints on the toys themselves, Auburn used all of these symbols, at one time or another, in their advertising.

MODELS AND MARKING

Auburn took pride in the realism of their rubber toy cars, trucks, and tractors. Not only were they designed to look like real models, in most cases they were actually advertised by a specific make and model and many were imprinted with the make and model.

The company always wanted to have the latest look to their toys and when they were able to get a toy on the market right away, they liked to use the actual model number. For example, the 1937 Oldsmobile appeared in their 1937 advertising and was proudly proclaimed "new 1937 Oldsmobile." The same ad carried the 1935 Fords but since they were already two model years old, they were simply referred to as "Fords." Two cars, the 1938 Oldsmobile and the 1939 Plymouth, were actually stamped underneath the running board with the make and model. The 1936 Cord, the 1937 Olds, and the 1940 Olds (early version), were marked with the make but not the model year.

Some cars, like the 1950 Cadillac and 1948 Buick, were not identified on the toy itself, but were clearly advertised by both make and model year in the Auburn catalogs. The only car that appears to be based on a real car but was never advertised by Auburn as such, is the 1946 Lincoln Zephyr convertible. It was simply listed as "convertible" in the catalog. Incidently, it was Auburn's first and only attempt at a rubber convertible, other than the Buick Y Job roadster.

The only old Auburn car that was not designed to look like a real car (or at least not like any real production car) was the futuristic, finned sedan that made its appearance in the Auburn line around 1949. This car has sort of a Buick-like grill and could be a pretty close copy of an actual GM dreamcar of the times. General Motors turned them out at a steady pace back then and it is hard to keep them all straight. Assuming it was a good likeness of a prototype model, Auburn lost all touch with reality by using it as an unlikely load on their authentic pre-war 1937 GMC car carrier — or even worse, as a fire chief's car in firetruck sets of the mid-fifties. This sleek car was the last new design by Auburn in real rubber and, along with a couple of rubber firetrucks, was the last rubber hold-out among a line that was almost completely vinyl in 1954.

All of Auburn's pre-war trucks were based on only two models — both very realistic. All of their stake trucks, in various sizes, were based on the 1937 International Metro cabovers. The tractor-trailer rigs were all based on the 1937 GMC cab-forward truck. After the war, these same trucks were made from old molds, until about 1949, when they started phasing in replacements for the beautiful old trucks. None of the replacements ever looked anything like a real truck and were referred to by Auburn as simply "large truck" or "small truck," etc.

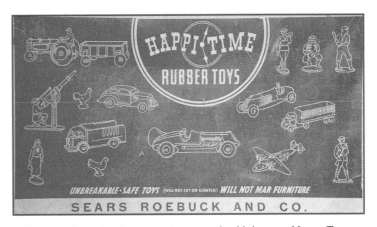

Sears packaged Auburn toys in sets and sold them as Happi Time Rubber Toys.

Photo courtesy of Dennis Dawson

Most of the post-war trucks were futuristic looking. The clear exception was the new pickup (Auburn's first pickup) introduced in 1950. It looks about like a 1950 pickup should look but for some unknown reason, they fitted it with wheels on the outside of the body. This created a bizarre look, not to mention the greater likelihood that some small kids would bite on the fully-exposed tires. They corrected the design the following year but I have never been able to figure out why they did it in the first place. Were they trying to use up overstocked axles that were too long for the truck?

COLORS

From the beginning, Auburn picked colors that were popular with kids and mostly stuck to some variations of red, blue, and green. I have only seen the Cord, the '37 and '38 Oldsmobiles, and some airplanes in silver. In 1940, they used orange as the fourth color, along with red, blue, and green. Red was always the dominant color. For example, the 1940 Oldsmobile was sold six red, two orange, two green, and two blue per dozen, according to the 1940 catalog. I believe orange was dropped after only one year.

The 1940 Oldsmobile was also available in a variety of two-toned combinations. It was done with the underside in white and the top, hood, and trunk in a darker color to simulate a taxi. A "taxi" decal was added to the front doors to complete the taxi version. The same car was also done in a simple two-tone, with only the roof painted a different color from the rest, in the style of real two-toned cars of the day. I have a dark blue car with a blue-gray top and I am sure there were other combinations.

The 1940 Olds is perhaps the vehicle that was offered in the most color combinations. It was done as a military medical car in khaki with a red cross on the top and as a military staff car in olive with army decals on the doors.

The 1940 Olds in the closed fender version (AA05) was sold in solid colors as well as very bright two-toned combinations of red on the bottom and bright yellow, blue, or green on the top half. To my knowledge, the only use of the color yellow by Auburn was limited to the two-toned versions of AA05, the Buick Sedanette (AA06), and some early tractors.

The most unusual combinations were offered on the 1938 Buick Y Job experimental roadster (advertised in the 1941 catalog as a 1941 Buick). This very large (almost 10 inches) car was offered in three different two-toned combinations. In the case of the green car, it was done in two shades of green — a dark green body with light green fenders. It was also offered as red or blue. I expect the blue version was done in a dark blue and a lighter blue-gray, like the 1940 Olds. It is hard to imagine how they painted a two-toned red, however.

Gray was used by Auburn in very modest amounts. Other than ships, which would have obviously been gray, and some trains, I have seen gray used only on 1935 Fords and 1937 Oldsmobiles.

White was used by Auburn for ambulances, milk trucks, and taxis as far as I can tell and even then, to a very limited degree. The milk truck appears in the 1940 catalog and the ambulance version of the International Metro appears in 1939 and 1940. The 1940 Olds taxi version appears in 1941. I do not have Auburn catalogs for every year but it is safe to assume that white is a very rare color.

I have seen the large pre-war racer in black. I have never seen another vehicle, other than locomotives, in black.

If you categorize colors as "general purpose" (cars, trucks, etc.) and "special purpose" (used only on certain specialized vehicles), I would rank the color scarcity as follows, with one being the most scarce:

General Purpose:

1. black	4. yellow	7. green
2. gray	5. orange	8. red
3. silver	6. blue	

Special Purpose:

1. white
2. khaki
3. olive

AA01
1936 Cord sedan,
6".
$70.00 – 150.00.

AA02
1937 Oldsmobile
four-door sedan,
4½".
$25.00 – 60.00.

AA02A
Variations include shape
of rear windows, trunk
handle, etc.

AA03
1938 Oldsmobile Six
two-door sedan,
5¾".
$50.00 – 100.00.

AA04
1940 Oldsmobile with open
fenders, civilian and
military versions,
6".
$35.00 – 65.00.

AA04
Taxi version
along with solid and
two-toned examples.

AA04
Taxi version.
Some creative kid long ago
glued a Disabled American
Veterans miniature license plate
(Penna. 1941) to the rear.

AA05
1940 Oldsmobile
with closed fenders,
6".
$30.00 – 50.00.

AA06
1948 Buick two-door sedanette,
7¼".
$50.00 – 100.00.

AA07
1938 Buick
Y Job experimental roadster,
9¾".
Rare.
From the Nelson Adams Collection

AA15
1938 Buick
Y Job experimental roadster,
9¾".
The original Y Job (AA07) included a driver
and was painted in two-toned combinations.
In an apparent cost-cutting effort, Auburn
eliminated the driver and switched to solid colors.
Rare.
Photo courtesy of Dick Ford

AA08 (bottom)
1935 Ford three-window coupe,
4".
$50.00 – 75.00.
AA09 (top)
1935 Ford two-door
slantback sedan,
4".
$50.00 – 75.00.

AA10
1950 Cadillac
four-door sedan,
7¼".
$50.00 – 100.00.

AA11
1939 Plymouth
two-door trunkback sedan,
4¼".
$35.00 – 55.00.

AA11
The Auburn 1939 Plymouth
used as a promotional. Imprint reads
"Your First Car From Joe E. Weber."
Photo courtesy of Dick Ford.

AA12 (left)
1946 Lincoln convertible,
4½",
with square headlights.
$20.00 – 40.00.

AA13 (right)
same, with round headlights.
$20.00 – 40.00.

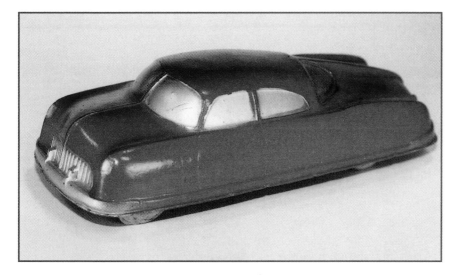

AA14
1949 futuristic sedan,
5".
$20.00 – 40.00.
Photo courtesy of Bill Ferretti

AA14A
The futuristic sedan came in two versions. AA14 has the number "A506" on the rear license plate, while AA14A has the number "506" on both front and rear plates, has much larger bumpers, other minor variations. Shown here are two AA14s with the AA14A on the left.

#564 Chevrolet Coupe

I only recently obtained a copy of the 1941 Auburn Rubber Company catalog, which included a car previously unknown to me. The 4¼" Chevrolet coupe is the same size as the AA02 1937 Olds, which is next to it. The toy appears in two places in the catalog, but unfortunately this old catalog has a blur across the front, which restricts the view of the grill and headlights. Based on this limited view, it appears to be a 1940 Chevrolet, although it could be a 1941 model. This toy does not appear in earlier catalogs and does not appear in postwar catalogs. I am inclined to say that Auburn did not publish a 1942 catalog, because of the war.

In all the years I have been collecting rubber toys, I have not seen this toy, nor have I known anyone that was aware of it. When I was doing basic research on the models Auburn made, I surveyed a lot of collectors and sometimes the feedback was confusing. For example, the 1937 Olds, we know as AA02, was reported to me by several collectors as a Buick or a Chevrolet. So, when I heard vague references to a "Chevrolet," I assumed they were mistakenly referring to AA02.

Now we have proof that the toy was manufactured. Or do we? Other toy makers have shown toys in their catalogs that were never actually produced. Auburn was pretty sloppy with their catalogs, as evidenced by their reference to a "Plymouth" on the same page, which we immediately recognize as the familiar Oldsmobile. If the toy was manufactured, it was probably offered for only one year, before toy production was shut down in 1942.

This little Chevrolet has just moved to the top of the list as the rarest Auburn of all. We christen it "AA16" and hope one turns up soon.

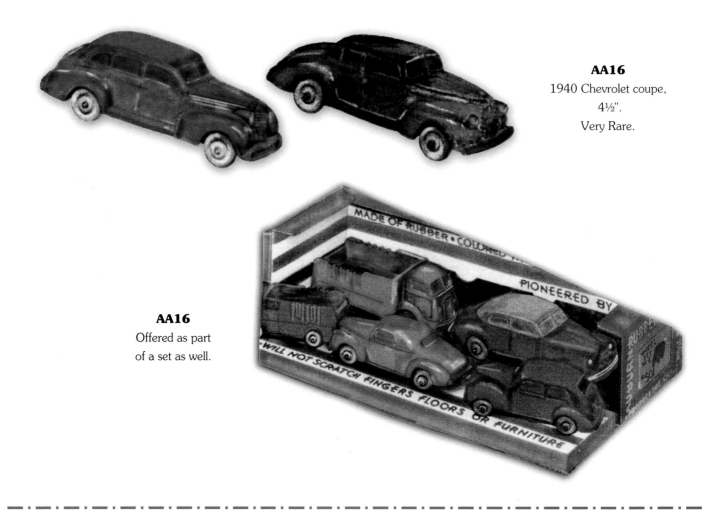

AA16
1940 Chevrolet coupe,
4½".
Very Rare.

AA16
Offered as part
of a set as well.

AT01

1937 International cabover,
5⅜",
with square front.
$30.00 – 60.00.

AT02

1937 International cabover,
5⅜",
with curved front, in civilian and
military versions.
$30.00 – 60.00.

AT02

Used as a promotional for
Allied Lines, Inc.
Photo courtesy of Dick Ford

AT03

1937 International cabover,
4¼",
with square front.
$20.00 – 40.00.

AT04
1937 International Metro cabover,
4¼",
with rounded front.
$20.00 – 40.00.

AT05
1937 International Metro cabover,
3⅞",
with square front.
$20.00 – 40.00.

The 1937 International cabover in three sizes.
AT01 (top), 5⅝"; AT03 (middle), 4¼";
AT05 (bottom), 3⅞".

AT06
1937 International cabover,
3⅞",
milk truck version.
Rare.

AT19
1937 International Metro cabover,
milk truck version,
4¼".
An Auburn catalog shows this truck with six
milk cans, but it will hold eight cans, as shown here.
Rare.

AT07
1937 International cabover,
5⅜",
ambulance version (top not original).
Rare.

AT08
1949 cab-forward box truck, futuristic,
5½".
$25.00 – 45.00.

AT09
1949 cabover box truck, futuristic,
4⅛".
$20.00 – 40.00.

AT10
1947 Chevrolet(?) box truck,
5½".
$25.00 – 45.00.

AT11 (left)
1950 pickup truck,
4½",
with wheels outside body.
$30.00 – 50.00.
AT12 (right)
same with wheels inside.
$20.00 – 40.00.

AT13
1937 GMC carry car,
11½",
shown with a box.
$65.00 – 95.00.
Photo courtesy of Bill Ferretti

AT14
1937 GMC carry car,
11½",
with cover on top.
$85.00 – 165.00.

AT14
Another view, which shows indentations that the car wheels fit into.

Photo courtesy of Bill Ferretti

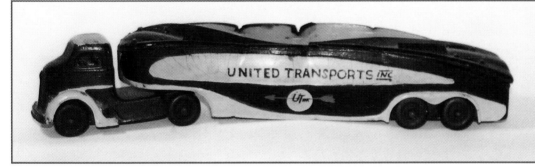

AT14
The carry car was used as a promotional for
United Transports, Inc.

*Photo courtesy of
Dick Ford*

AT17
1950 carry car,
11⅞",
trailer is the same but the
tractor has been modernized.
$65.00 – 100.00.

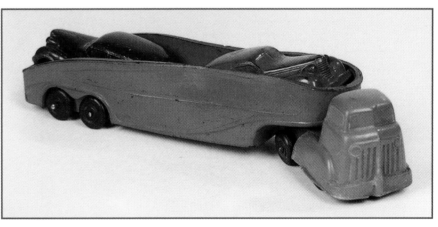

AT15
1937 GMC tractor with stake trailer,
9",
with built-in tailgate.
$65.00 – 105.00.

AT16
1937 GMC cab
with stake trailer,
9",
with moveable tail gate.
$65.00 – 100.00.

AT16 (right)
1937 GMC tractor
with stake trailer,
9",
with moveable tailgate
(missing here).
AT15 (left)
AT18
1935 Ford stake truck
4¾".
Very Rare.
No photo available.

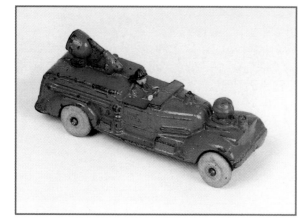

AE01
Ahrens-Fox fire engine,
5½".
$60.00 – 150.00.

AE02
Hose and ladder truck,
7¾".
$35.00 – 55.00.

AE03
Fire pumper,
with boiler,
7¾".
$35.00 – 55.00.

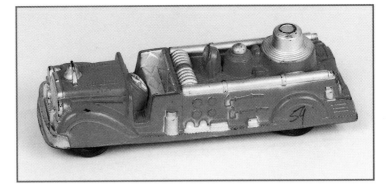

AE04 (left)
Ladder truck, no hose,
7¾".
$45.00 – 75.00.
AE05 (right)
is the same truck with
hose crank.
Rare.
Photo courtesy of Bill Ferretti

AE05
Shown here with a shoestring simulating a hose. This version was more realistic but the crank was held in place by two staples and easily removed (and lost).
Photo courtesy of Dick Ford

AE02
As it came straight from the mold. Flashing would have been trimmed by hand, buffed on a wheel, and then sent to be painted.
Photo courtesy of Bill Ferretti

Auburn Fire Station. This set was offered late in the rubber era of Auburn. The futuristic sedan was the only rubber car remaining in their line, so they used it as a fire chief's car. Note motorcycle and firefighters are vinyl.

Photo courtesy of Dennis Dawson

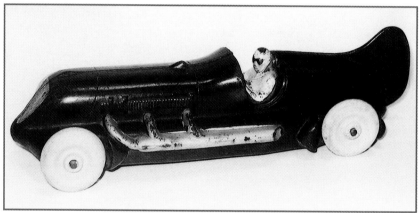

AR01
Open Racer,
10½".
$75.00 – 150.00.
Photo courtesy of Ron Snow

Auburn's first large racer (AR01) was sold at Indianapolis as a souvenir from the racetrack. This photo shows the words "Indianapolis" and "Wilbur Shaw" hand written in gold ink on the hood of the racer. Wilbur Shaw won the Indianapolis 500 in 1937, 1939, and 1940 and was the first driver to win in two consecutive years.

AR02
Open racer,
10½".
$65.00 – 95.00.

AR03
Open racer,
10½".
$45.00 – 75.00.

AR04
Open racer,
6½",
shown here in
Auburn's three favorite colors.
$30.00 – 55.00.

AR05
Open racer,
4¾".
$22.00 – 45.00.

AR06
Open racer,
6¼".
$25.00 – 45.00.

AR07
Open racer,
6½".
$50.00 – 80.00.
Photo courtesy of Ron Snow

AR08
Open racer,
5¼".
$25.00 – 40.00.

AR09
Open racer,
4¾".
$35.00 – 60.00.

AR10
Red Devil racer,
5⅞",
Very rare.
Photo courtesy of Bill Ferretti

AF01
Farm tractor,
John Deere A.,
5".
$30.00 – 50.00.

AF02
Farm tractor,
Minneapolis-Moline Z,
4".
$30.00 – 50.00.

AF03
Farm tractor,
Minneapolis-Moline R,
8".
$65.00 – 100.00.

AF03
An early model in yellow paint.
Photo courtesy of Bill Ferretti

AF04
Farm tractor, Minneapolis Moline R,
7⅜".
This toy is new old stock from an old
hardware store and has the original Kruse
Hardware tag and the $1.00 price.
$60.00 – 90.00.
Photo courtesy of Ron Snow

AF05
Farm Tractor,
Oliver Row Crop,
6½".
$80.00 – 120.00.
Photo courtesy of BIll Ferretti

AF05
Shown in the rare green color.
Look closely to see other differences in
the red and green tractors.

AF06
Farm tractor,
McCormick-Deering IH
Farmall M,
4".
$30.00 – 50.00.

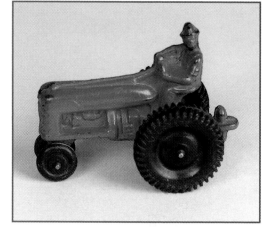

AF07
Farm tractor,
Graham-Bradley,
4¼".
$45.00 – 75.00.

AF08
Farm tractor,
4".
This toy is common in the vinyl version
and for years I held the belief that it
was never made in a rubber version.
Bob Howard convinced me otherwise
with this excellent photo.
Rare.

AI01
Graham-Bradley,
two-wheel trailer,
5¾".
$45.00 – 65.00.

AI02
Graham-Bradley,
four-wheel trailer,
4¾".
$30.00 – 50.00.

AI03
Thresher (Harvester),
5½".
$55.00 – 110.00.
Photo courtesy of Ron Snow

AI03
This example belongs to Dennis Dawson and is unusually straight. This toy is usually found with the chute missing or badly sagging.

AI04 (left)
David Bradley spreader,
4¾".
$20.00 – 40.00.
AI05 (right)
Spreader,
4¾".
$20.00 – 40.00.

AI06
Reliable front lift seeder
(grain drill),
3".
$25.00 – 45.00.
Photo courtesy of Bill Ferretti

AI07
David Bradley sickle sidebar cutter,
3".
$25.00 – 45.00.

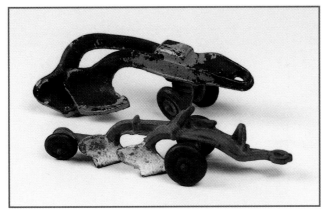

AI08 (bottom)
David Bradley plow,
4¾".
$25.00 – 45.00.
AI09 (top)
Two-wheel plow,
4¾".
$20.00 – 40.00.

AI10
David Bradley cultipacker,
4⅛".
$30.00 – 60.00.
Photo courtesy of Bill Ferretti

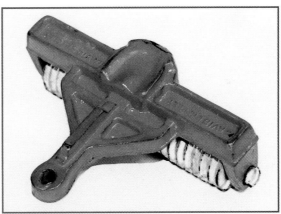

AI11
Harrow, no moving parts,
4½".
Rare.
No photo available.
AI12
David Bradley disc harrow,
2½".
$30.00 – 60.00.
Photo courtesy of Bill Ferretti

AI13
Plow seeder,
3½".
$60.00 – 120.00.
Photo courtesy of Bill Ferretti

AI14
Blade,
2¾",
fits Graham-Bradley tractor.
Rare.

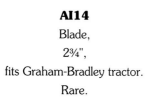

AI16
Hay rake,
2¾",
fits Graham-Bradley tractor. Today, most hay
is cut and bailed in a single operation. In earlier
days, hay may have been cut by one machine,
pushed into piles, using a device such as this,
and then fed into a hay bailer.
Rare.

AI16
Shown with a beautiful orange
Graham-Bradley tractor.
Photo courtesy of Charley Maledon

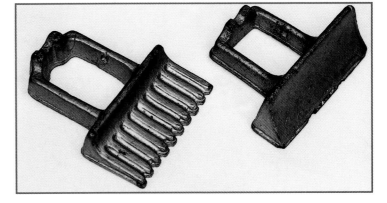

AI14 and AI16
Detailed comparison.
Photo courtesy of Bill Ferretti

AI15
David Bradley hay wagon,
5".
$60.00 – 100.00.
Photo courtesy of Ron Snow

A beautiful farm set any kid would have loved,
and today, any collector would love even more.
Photo courtesy of Ron Snow

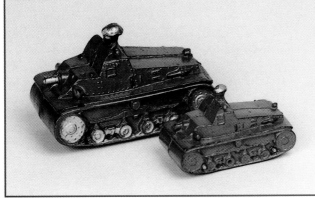

AM01 (top)
Marmon-Harrington tank,
4½".
$30.00 – 50.00.
AM02 (bottom)
Marmon-Harrington tank,
3⅛".
$25.00 – 40.00.

AM01

Tank in normal version (right) and headless version (left). This may have been a deliberate design change by Auburn or could be simply a defective toy that escaped the inspectors.

AM02

Was produced in a double-axle version (right), and a single-axle version (left).

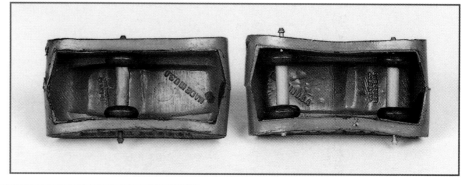

AM03 (right)

155 MM Howitzer,
6¾".
$20.00 – 30.00.

AM05 (left)

75MM field piece,
7¾".
$20.00 – 30.00.

Photo courtesy of Bill Ferretti

AM04

75MM Field Piece,
6".
This is a redesigned version of AM05. The original field piece was longer and vulnerable to breaking off. Today, collectors find many with the barrel broken off. My guess is that Auburn created this version with a stubby barrel, which would be less realistic, but more sturdy.
$20.00 – 30.00.

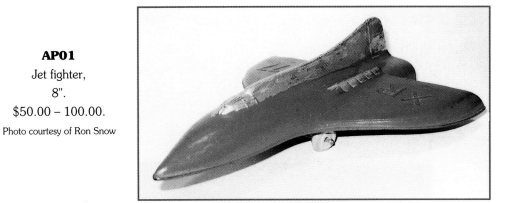

AP01
Jet fighter,
8".
$50.00 – 100.00.
Photo courtesy of Ron Snow

AP02
Jet fighter,
4½".
$30.00 – 40.00.

AP03
Curtiss P-37 pursuit plane,
3½"
(prop not original).
$35.00 – 55.00.

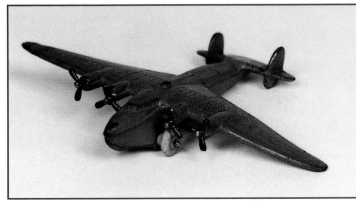

AP04
Boeing C-98 Clipper,
5½"
(props not original).
$50.00 – 75.00.

AP05
Douglas DC-2 transport,
4⅝"
(props not original).
$45.00 – 70.00.

AP06
Consolidated A-11 light bomber,
3½"
(prop not original).
$35.00 – 55.00.

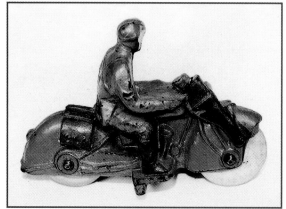

AC01
Motorcycle Scout,
3⅞".
$50.00 – 100.00.
Photo courtesy of Bill Ferretti

AC02
Motorcycle with sidecar gunner,
3¼".
$50.00 – 125.00.
Photo courtesy of Bill Ferretti

AC02

Compared to a similar metal toy
made by Barclay.

Photo courtesy of Ron Snow

AC03 (left)
Motorcycle with cop,
3⅞".
$50.00 – 80.00.
AC04 (right)
Motorcycle with cop,
5".
$90.00 – 150.00.

AC03

Shown in military and civilian versions.

Photo courtesy of Bill Ferretti

AB01
Submarine,
6½".
$30.00 – 50.00.

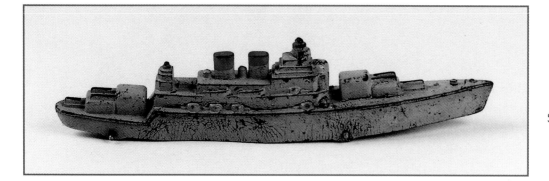

AB02
Battleship,
8¼".
$40.00 – 60.00.

AB03
Battleship (Dreadnaught),
9⅛".
$40.00 – 60.00.

AB04
Freighter,
9¼".
$50.00 – 75.00.

AN01

Steam locomotive,

9¾".

$45.00 – 75.00.

AN02

Train set, locomotive, dump car,

gondola, and caboose,

27".

The locomotive was sold

separately, but the cars were not.

$90.00 – 150.00.

AN03

Engine and tender,

11",

in the closed version in black.

$50.00 – 80.00.

AN09

The same engine with an open

tender. This AN09, in gray, bears

the number "999."

$50.00 – 80.00.

Photo courtesy of Bill Ferretti

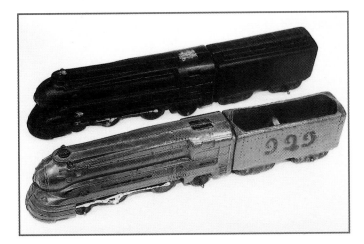

AN09

This is AN09 in another version

with "777" on the tender.

Photo courtesy of Ron Snow

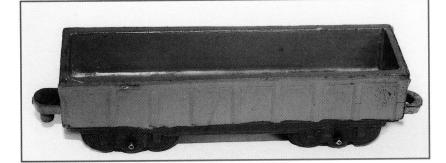

AN04

Gondola car,

5½".

$25.00 – 40.00.

Photo courtesy of Bill Ferrretti

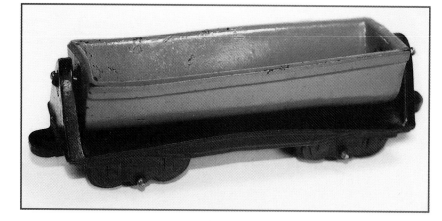

AN05
Dump car,
5½".
$25.00 – 40.00.
Photo courtesy of Bill Ferretti

AN06
Caboose,
4½".
$25.00 – 40.00.
Photo courtesy of Bill Ferretti

AN07
Crane car,
5".
Rare.
Photo courtesy of Bill Ferretti

AN08
Freight engine and tender,
11".
This engine pulled the
same cars as AN03.
Rare.
Photo courtesy of Steve Kelley

COMPOSITION TOYS

World War II required much of American industry to focus on fighting the war and strategic materials like steel, aluminum, and rubber could not be used to make toys.

American kids still wanted toys, of course, which led toymakers to look for other materials that could be used. Wood and paper were obvious choices and many toys were made from those materials. Auburn experimented with many compounds that were on the list of non-essential materials. They tried excelsior and lime, soybean flour, and even old battery cases, with little success. The limited success they did achieve was with a composition of essentially sawdust and glue.

Other companies had used a similar compound for years — long before the war — to make dolls. Some toy companies used the composition material to mold soldiers, planes, ships, and other toys during the war years. Auburn did produce some vehicles, with limited success, but was not satisfied with the quality and eventually gave up toy production altogether until the war ended.

The vehicles you see here are not marked in any way to identify them as Auburn, however, their striking resemblance to the rubber 39 Plymouth and the International Metro cabover is proof enough for me. Also, the white rubber tires on these composition vehicles are identical to those used by Auburn on other rubber toys of the era.

This little Plymouth and Metro are the only composition toys I have seen and I have seen them only in red. These toys were made in limited quantities and are fragile, so Auburn toy collectors face a serious challenge in locating examples of these rare toys.

Plastic Toys

During the early fifties, Auburn management realized that plastic would eventually replace rubber as a material for toys and began gearing up for the transition. They wanted the toy to be flexible and rubber-like, so their early experiments with hard plastic were not successful. They eventually found what they were looking for in vinyl.

The first vinyl toys were offered in 1953, and by 1956 all rubber vehicles had been replaced by vinyl. The first vinyl toys introduced by Auburn were the large racer (#536) and the small motorcycle cop (#520). These were thick, high-quality toys, with black rubber tires and even today collectors often mistake them for rubber toys. Unfortunately, over the years, continued cost-cutting decisions resulted in a flimsy toy that fell far short of the traditional Auburn standard of quality.

During the sixties, following the move to Deming, New Mexico, Auburn made hard plastic toys that represent a further decline in quality.

THE SUN RUBBER COMPANY

In 1923, three men in McKeesport, Pennsylvania, became interested in a process owned by an Englishman, for making hard rubber radio panels. They purchased the bankrupt Avalon Rubber Company plant in Barberton, Ohio, a suberb of Akron, for the purpose of manufacturing the radio panels. The process turned out to be worthless and they decided to try to recoup their investment by putting the plant on a paying basis with some other product.

On April 4, 1923, The Sun Rubber Company was founded, with John T. McLane, president, Joseph L. McLane, vice president, and T.W. Smith, Jr., as secretary and treasurer. Mr. Smith moved to Barberton and assumed the duties of general manager as well. They looked around for a product to produce and came up with a doll-sized hot water bottle. In 1924, they landed their first order with Woolworth for 100,000 of these tiny hot water bottles mounted on cardboard, and the Sun Rubber Company was off and running!

Following their initial success, Sun added a small inflated rubber doll to their line and continued to expand during the late twenties and early thirties. By 1932, they were producing a fast-selling teething ring, several varieties of dolls, and doll accessories, such as bath sets.

On November 2, 1934, Sun filed a patent for a rubber toy automobile, which featured a unique design for the axles and wheels. The prototype for this first toy auto was a 1934 DeSoto Airflow and was introduced to the public in their 1935 advertisement which announced Sun's toy line as "Dolls, animals, and autos." The first toy auto was offered in a choice of five colors: red, blue, green, yellow, and gray (which we would more likely think of as silver), and was marked "patent applied for" underneath. On March 24, 1936, the U.S. Patent Office issued patent number 2,035,081 for the Sun Rubber design. Thereafter, Sun products bore this patent number.

The 1936 catalog offered a wide variety of dolls and doll accessories and the original DeSoto Airflow was joined by seven other vehicles: a coupe, a larger teardrop sedan, two trucks, a streamlined bus, and two open racers. The company flourished during the late thirties as they continued to add varieties to their toy line. In 1938, they reached an agreement with Warner Brothers to produce Porky Pig and later negotiated similar arrangements with Walt Disney for production of Mickey Mouse and other cartoon characters.

During the pre-war era, The Sun Rubber Company employed around 500 employees at its Barberton plant and T.W. Smith continued to provide outstanding leadership for the manufacturing operation. Mr. Smith was well respected throughout the toy industry and twice served as president of the Toy Manufacturers of the U.S.A., Inc.

Wartime brought an end to toy products in Barberton but the modern plant was put to good use in the manufacture of defense products. Sun was a leading manufacturer of oxygen masks, respirators, and rubber fittings for aircraft and aircrews. Sun was a key player in the development of synthetic rubber technology during the war and was especially noted for developing rubber/metal clad products, such as bullet-resistant fuel cells for aircraft. Wartime employment at the plant reached 1200.

The War Department negotiated with Sun Rubber to manufacture a special gas mask for children, in the event the United States was invaded and gas became a threat. The mask was personally designed by Walt Disney and took the shape of the famous Mickey Mouse, ears and all! The mask was never produced in significant quantities and today represents the ultimate Disney collectible.

Following the war, Sun Rubber quickly turned war production back into toy production. They started producing many of the old favorites from before the war, and introduced new models as well. In a June 1946 press release, Sun introduced a new army tank and scout car "made from the same synthetic rubber as the bullet-sealing gas tanks." Despite high production, Sun was unable to meet consumer demands and filled orders on the basis of pre-war business, which meant that many retail outlets were not able to get the toys they wanted. Business was very good during the late forties and T.W. Smith continued as general manager. In 1951, Mr. Smith became chairman, president, and treasurer of the company.

The late fifties and early sixties were turbulent years for Sun, as they felt the pressure from foreign imports and the economy sagged all over the country. Barberton was hit by loss of employment and the rubber toy companies could not match the wages and benefits that the tire industry could offer to rubber workers. Union relations were difficult, at best.

ANTIQUE TOY ANTICS   BY JOHN WEST

THE SUN RUBBER COMPANY
BARBERTON, OHIO

72

To Dave Leopard with Best Wishes and
Good Luck! John West 11-15-97

On March 12, 1960, Sun announced that they had secured $2,750,000 in new financing and was stepping up production. Sun invested heavily in vinyl technology and many court battles were waged over patents on their process for rotational casting of vinyl products. Further refinancing and reorganization during 1966 led to a change in the name of the company to the "Sun Corporation." During the sixties, the company switched the emphasis of its product line to sporting goods and later to interior trim for automobiles and other vinyl products for the auto industry.

On June 19, 1969, Sun became a wholly owned subsidiary of Talley Industries. In 1971, the Barberton plant was closed by a strike after 51 years of operation. Several years of negotiations failed to produce a union contract that would allow the plant to reopen. Some Sun product lines were moved to another Talley plant in Carrollton, Georgia, and the Barberton plant was permanently closed on April 20, 1974. It is difficult to pinpoint exactly when the original Sun Rubber Company went out of business, because of the various name changes, mergers, and evolutionary changes in their product line. My interest in the company, as a collector of rubber toy vehicles, really focused more on when they made those products, as opposed to when they were in business. Sun introduced the first rubber vehicle in 1935 and the last year a rubber wheel toy was listed in their catalog was 1955. That's about 20 years in the rubber toy business, during which they produced some 32 different varieties of vehicles, with hundreds of color variations.

March 24, 1936   M. S. LOWER   2,035,081

TOY AUTOMOBILE

Filed Nov. 2, 1934

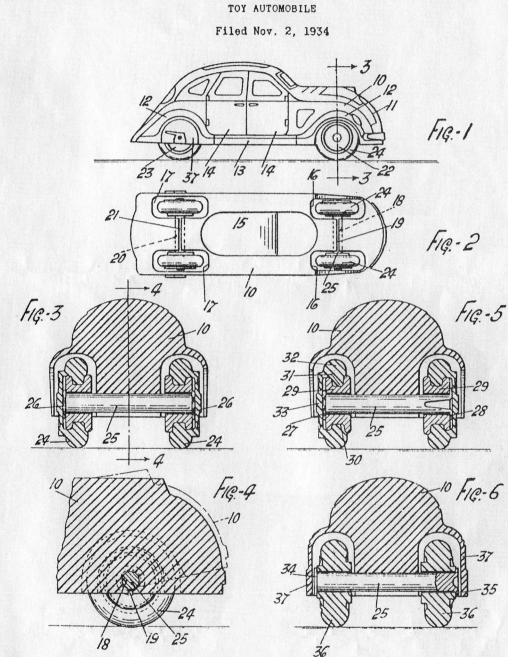

INVENTOR
MELVIN S. LOWER

BY

Albert L. Ely

ATTORNEY

MODELS AND MARKING

Sun was very conservative in adding or deleting toys in the product line. They seemed to follow the general philosophy that new models should be selected with great care and once in the line should remain for as long as they continued to sell. They reinforced that philosophy by guarding against built-in obsolescence associated with very specific make and model designs. Auburn, for example, liked to have very well detailed models in their line but no kid is going to want a 1935 Ford for many years after car designs have drastically changed. On the other hand, Sun introduced its supercharged coupe in 1936 and continued selling it through 1952, perhaps later. Since the coupe was not based on any specific car model and it had a sort of sporty appeal that does not diminish over time, it was not viewed as out-of-date by toy buyers.

Sun's first toy automobile, a 1934 DeSoto Airflow, was introduced to the public in 1935. The toy was marked "PAT APPLIED FOR" underneath in the center. Underneath one running board was embossed "The Sun Rubber Co., Barberton, O. USA." The opposite running board bore the mark "ALL RUBBER." The solid, white rubber tires were embossed to simulate artillery wheels of the time and bore the name, "Sunruco" along the tire wall.

Sun apparently dropped the "ALL RUBBER" marking very quickly, since it does not appear on any model other than the original Airflow. The Sunruco tires were soon replaced by smooth tires. Only the Airflow, Teardrop sedan (SA04), and the large stake body truck (ST02) have been observed with Sunruco tires.

The Sun patent was not issued until March 24, 1936, but Sun continued to add new vehicles to the line prior to that date. Several of the small vehicles may be found marked "Patent Pending," indicating they are 1935 or early 1936 products. After the patent was issued, all Sun vehicles bore the familiar patent number 2,035,081.

Following are six early vehicles that were dropped from the line before the war:

1. The '34 DeSoto Airflow (SA02) was replaced by the '40 Dodge sedan (SA03).
2. The pickup truck (ST01) was replaced by the futuristic open truck (ST03).
3. The larger, stake body truck (ST02) was replaced by the large, futuristic truck that Sun called the "Master" truck (ST05).
4. The original large racer (SR02) was replaced by the new "Super" racer (SR03).
5. The house trailer (SA05) was dropped and not replaced.
6. The town car (SA06) was dropped and not replaced.

Fourteen of the pre-war vehicles were again produced in new colors following the war. Nine of the fourteen were continued in the Sun line until they dropped wheel toys altogether around 1953 or 1954.

In 1947, Sun introduced six new toys: the tank, scout car, Mickey Mouse tractor, Mickey Mouse fire truck, Mickey Mouse airplane, and Donald Duck roadster. These would prove to be the last new toy vehicles introduced by Sun.

Sun dropped several vehicles in 1949, including the small, futuristic truck, the ambulance, all of the airplanes, and the tank and scout car, which had been in the line for only two years.

In 1951, renewed interest in war toys, brought on by the Korean War, caused Sun to bring back the tank, scout car, small truck, ambulance, and two of the airplanes. They were all done in olive with silver trim.

The early fifties saw Sun's vehicles go away, as they concentrated more on dolls and sports equipment. The four Disney vehicles continued in the Sun line through 1955 and then they passed from the scene as well.

COLORS

The original Sun auto, a 1934 DeSoto Airflow, was offered in red, blue, green, yellow, and gray (silver). Sun vehicles in the 1936 catalog were painted in solid colors, according to the perceived childhood preferences of the day. The choice of colors indicates an overwhelming preference for red, with nine of each dozen toys painted in red. Two green and one blue completed the dozen. In the pre-war years that followed, they continued to use yellow and silver, although neither color is included in the 1936 catalog.

Somewhere around World War II (just before or just after), Sun switched over to two-toned combinations. Most models made the transition and are found today in the full range of solid colors and many two-toned varieties as well. The toys that are found only in solid colors, like the town car (SA06) or the streamlined pickup truck (ST01), were dropped from the line before the transition to the two-toned toys began.

The two-toned toys were usually done with a dark color (red, blue, green) on the bottom and a lighter color (yellow, gray, beige) on the top. Of course, there were variations in shades over the years, which produced many possible combinations. The trucks were sometimes done in a combination of silver and another color. The small racers were painted a solid light color, with the numbers and tail fin painted in contrasting dark colors.

Sun used khaki paint to militarize a few vehicles prior to World War II. As the Korean War brought military toys to the forefront again, many of the same toys were re-done in olive green with silver trim. Unlike Auburn, Sun did not use decals. Stars and other military markings were applied with silver paint.

SA01
1936 supercharged coupe,
4",
in post-war (two-toned), and
pre-war (solid color) versions.
$30.00 – 50.00.

SA01
The supercharged coupe was
one of three cars sometimes
equipped with a trailer hitch.
The others are SA05 and SA06.

SA02
1934 DeSoto Airflow sedan,
4".
$30.00 – 50.00.

SA02
The little Airflow was used as a
promotional. The decal reads,
"Auto Loans at Lower Cost
Home State Bank 6th and Minn."
Photo courtesy of Dick Ford

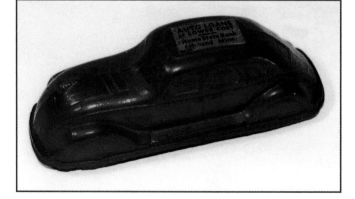

SA03

1940 Dodge four-door sedan,
4½".
Shown alongside a Japanese
salt and pepper shaker, which
was modeled after the toy.
$30.00 – 50.00.

SA03

Shown is the rare convertible
version. This one was custom made by
the author at age 12.

SA03

These sedans have been stripped of paint to
show the difference in raw material used by Sun.
The gray, speckled version is pre-war natural rubber,
while the black sedan is made from post-war
synthetic rubber.

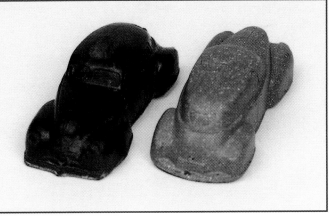

SA04

1936 Teardrop sedan,
5½".
$35.00 – 55.00.

SA05
House trailer,
4⅜".
Rare.

SA06
1936 town car (Brewster Limo),
5⅜".
$80.00 – 120.00.

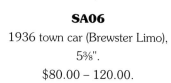

SA07
1937 station wagon,
3¾",
in civilian and military versions.
$30.00 – 50.00.

ST01
1936 stake-side pickup truck,
4¼".
$30.00 – 50.00.

ST02

1936 White stake-side truck,
5¼".
$45.00 – 85.00.

ST03

Tractor/trailer, three axles,
5⅛".
$30.00 – 50.00.

ST04

Futuristic open truck,
4½",
in civilian and military versions.
$30.00 – 50.00.

ST05

Master truck,
5⅝".
$35.00 – 55.00.

ST06
1936 White bus,
4¼".
$30.00 – 50.00.

ST07
1937 ambulance,
3¾",
in civilian and
military versions.
$30.00 – 50.00.

SR01
Open racer,
4⅜".
Pre-war versions were solid
colored, had no numbers, and had
small white tires. The post-war version
had numbers, painted trim, and are found
with both black and white tires in large
and small sizes.
$30.00 – 50.00.

SR02
Open racer,
6½",
is loosely based on the famous
German Auto Union racers.
$60.00 – 90.00.

SR03

Open racer,
6¾".
$40.00 – 70.00.

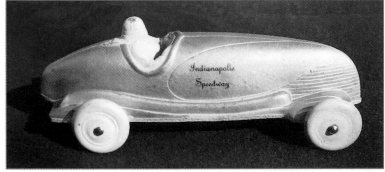

SR03

The racer was sold as a souvenir
at the Indianapolis Speedway.

SR03

The versatile racer was also used as a
souvenir of the Soap Box Derby.

Photo courtesy of Charley Maledon

SR03

The All American Soap Box Derby, Akron, Ohio.

Photo courtesy of Carl Natter

SM01
Tank,
6".
$40.00 – 60.00.

SM02 (right)
Scout car,
6¾",
with roller.
$40.00 – 60.00.
SM03 (left)
without the roller.
$40.00 – 60.00.

SP01
Transport aircraft,
4"
(props not original).
$30.00 – 50.00.

SP02 (left)
Pursuit ship,
3".
$25.00 – 45.00.
SP03
(not marked pursuit),
in military and
civilian versions.
Note original price 19¢.
$25.00 – 45.00.

SP02

This little plane served as a souvenir of Pensacola, Florida, "The Annapolis of the Air." Pensacola has long served as the base for Naval Aviation training. Too bad Sun did not make an aircraft carrier, so we could practice our landings.

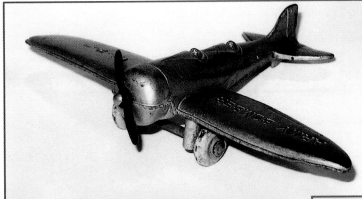

SP04

Army bomber,
4½".
$30.00 – 65.00.

Photo courtesy of Ron Snow

SD01

Mickey Mouse tractor,
4¾"
(SD05 is identical tractor with Donald Duck head).
$70.00 – 150.00.

SD02

Mickey Mouse fire truck,
6¾"
(SD06 is identical fire truck with Donald Duck head).
$60.00 – 120.00.

SD03
Mickey Mouse airplane,
6¼"
(SD07 is identical airplane
with Donald Duck head).
$70.00 – 150.00.
Photo courtesy Bill Ferretti

The underside of Bill Ferretti's Mickey
Mouse airplane bears the original Woolworth
price tag — 79 cents.

SD04
Donald Duck roadster,
6½"
(SD08 is identical roadster
with Mickey Mouse head).
$60.00 – 120.00.

Sun Rubber Auto-Aero Set original box.

Photo courtesy of Larry Forte

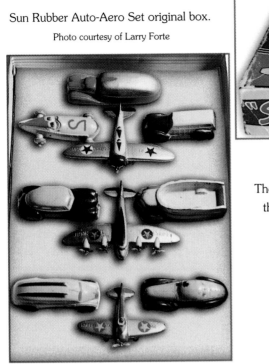

The Auto-Aero contents. Note that Sun used metal props on their aircraft, unlike Auburn, who used rubber props. The metal ones have a far greater chance of surviving.

Photo courtesy of Carl Natter

WEE WHEELS

The Sun Rubber Company did not produce rubber toys after the plant was closed in Barberton, Ohio. They did make at least one attempt to remain in the toy business after the company was moved to Georgia. These Wee Wheels are made of vinyl and bear little resemblance to the Sun rubber toys that preceded them. Printing on the toy is as follows:

Wee Wheels
Sun Products Corporation
Carrollton, Georgia 30117
A Talley Industries Company

THE RAINBOW RUBBER COMPANY

Little is known about the Rainbow Rubber Company of Butler, Pennsylvania, except that they made some beautifully detailed rubber toy vehicles around 1935. Neither a catalog nor an advertisement has surfaced, which would provide insight into the company or its product line.

Only six vehicles have been cataloged as Rainbow toys and they all appear to be 1935 models. The toys are clearly marked "MFG'D BY RAINBOW RUBBER CO. BUTLER, PA.," and the cars are all marked "OLDSMOBILE." They are also marked with the trademark "RUBRTOY," which is sometimes mistaken by collectors as "AUBRTOY" and therefore thought to be made by the Auburn Rubber Company. Auburn never used the name "AUBRTOY" on their toys but it remains a source of confusion.

Rainbow used white rubber tires that were embossed to simulate the popular artillery wheels of the era. The axle is a round-headed, nickel plated nail that serves as a hubcap as well.

RA01
1935 Oldsmobile coupe,
3¾".
$50.00 – 80.00.

RA02
1935 Oldsmobile sedan,
3¼".
$50.00 – 80.00.

RA03
1935 Oldsmobile sedan,
5".
$65.00 – 125.00.

RA02 (bottom)
1935 Oldsmobile
four-door sedan,
3¼".
RA03 (top)
1935 Oldsmobile
four-door sedan,
5".

RT01
1935 Studebaker
stake-body pickup truck,
5¼".
$50.00 – 80.00.

RR01 (bottom)
Open racer,
4".
$35.00 – 55.00.
RR02 (top)
Open racer,
5".
Rare.
Photo courtesy of Bill Ferretti

THE BARR RUBBER PRODUCTS COMPANY

The Barr Rubber Products Company of Sandusky, Ohio, advertised itself as the "World's Largest Manufacturer of Toy Balloons" in 1935. We know they made other rubber playthings as well, including some outstanding toy 1935 Fords.

The only Barr advertisement we have uncovered is this one from the November 1935 issue of *Playthings* magazine, a publication for toy buyers. This ad states that they offer "four different models," while the illustration shows only three. We are assuming the fourth model is a stake truck. We are further assuming that the ambulance variation of the panel truck and the army variation of the stake truck were produced by Barr as well.

This ad from a May-June 1936 Butler Brothers catalog includes a full line of rubber Fords, but does not identify the manufacturer. We believe they are Barr. Note that the ambulance and army truck are photographs, while the other models are sketches, which could indicate that the ambulance and army truck were added to the line after the original ad had been laid out. Note also that the sedan is shown in smaller scale than the others and is the only one that does not say "black rubber wheels." In fact, the illustration depicts the sedan with white tires. This is but a part of the mystery surrounding the small rubber 1935 Fords, discussed in a later chapter.

BA01
1935 Ford
three-window coupe,
4".
$35.00 – 70.00.

BA02
1935 Ford
slantback sedan,
4".
$35.00 – 70.00.

BT01 (right)
1935 Ford
stake-body truck,
4¾".
$35.00 – 70.00.
BT03 (left)
1935 Ford
army truck,
4¾".
$45.00 – 90.00.

BT01

A promotional for "B. Altman
and Co. East Orange, N. J."

BT02

1935 Ford
panel truck,
4¼",
and ambulance version.
$35.00 – 70.00.

FIRESTONE FORDS

The Firestone Tire and Rubber Company installed a giant press in the Ford exhibit building at the San Diego World's Fair in 1935 and manufactured souvenir, rubber toy Ford Tudors, which they sold to fairgoers for a dime.

Firestone continued the practice in 1936 at the Great Lakes Exposition in Cleveland and the Texas Centennial in Dallas. The Cleveland and Texas Fords were 1936 Tudors, very similar to the 1935 model, the primary difference being the grill design.

In 1939, they set up a press at the Golden Gate Exposition in San Francisco and molded 1939 Mercury four-door sedans.

All of these Firestone Fords were done in exquisite detail. The white rubber tires were embossed with the Firestone logo and mounted on red wooden hubs. The wheels were held in place with nickel-plated, nail-like axles, whose head formed a rounded hubcap. The cars were offered in a wide variety of colors and were individually boxed.

FA01
1939 Mercury
four-door sedan,
4¾".
$80.00 – 200.00.

FA01
A bright yellow version.
Photo courtesy of Ron Snow

FA02
1935 Ford,
two-door
trunkback sedan,
4⅞".
$80.00 – 200.00.
Photo courtesy of Gates & Evelyn Willard

A very well-cared-for souvenir of
the California Pacific Exposition.
Photo courtesy of Ron Snow

The San Diego Fords in three colors.
Photo courtesy Dick Ford

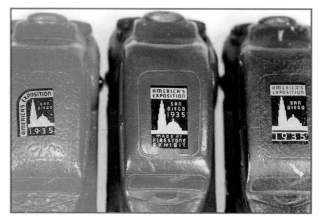

Three different decals used at
the San Diego Exposition.
Photo courtesy of Bill Ferretti

FA03
1936 Ford
two-door trunkback sedan,
4⅞".
$80.00 – 200.00.
Photo courtesy of Gates & Evelyn Willard

Three beautiful Cleveland
1936 Fords, with three
different style roof decals.
Photo courtesy of Dick Ford

FA03
From the Texas Centennial in Dallas.
Photo courtesy of Ron Snow

THE BRITISH EMPIRE EXHIBITION

In 1924, the British Empire covered over one-quarter of the land on Earth, but World War I and the crushing unemployment that followed, took a terrible toll.

The Empire Exhibition was designed to stimulate trade, to strengthen the bonds that tied the Mother Country and her Sister States and Daughter Nations, to bring all into closer touch, one with the other, to enable all who owe allegiance to the British Flag to meet on common ground and to learn about each other.

The Exhibition in England in 1924 – 25 was followed in later years by smaller exhibitions around the Empire. The Empire Exhibition in Johannesburg, South Africa, was held in 1936 – 37 and Firestone was on hand to stamp out little rubber 1936 Fords, just as they had done in Cleveland and Dallas. The Ford appears to be exactly like those produced in the United States, except the printing underneath, which reads, "Empire Exhibition South Africa 1936."

Photo courtesy of Bill Ferretti

Seiberling Latex Products Company

The Seiberling Latex Products Company was located in Barberton, Ohio, a suburb of Akron, and is not to be confused with the company that made tires. This company entered the rubber toy business in 1931 with parts for large dolls and later produced smaller dolls. They began making rubber toy autos in 1934 but apparently did not stay in the doll or auto business very long. According to an article in the *Barberton Herald* on November 25, 1938, "much of the doll and automobile business has been lost to firms outside of this industrial area because of labor costs."

Seiberling achieved its greatest success with the exclusive rights to produce certain rubber cartoon characters, particularly those from Walt Disney. In addition to the Disney characters Mickey Mouse, Donald Duck, Pluto, the Three Little Pigs, Snow White and the Seven Dwarfs, and Ferdinand the Bull, they also made Popeye and Wimpy.

Golden Gate Ford.
Photo courtesy of Dick Ford

Seiberling turned out a very realistic 1935 Ford two-door slantback sedan, in two sizes, four inches and just under five inches. The toys are well marked with "Seiberling Latex Prod. Co. Akron, Ohio" under one running board and "All Rubber Made in U.S.A." under the other running board. They also have "Ford" imprinted under the front bumper. The tires are smooth white rubber donuts, mounted on green wooden hubs.

These are the only two vehicles that have positively been identified as Seiberlings. They may have made some other models of the small 1935 Fords (similar to those of Barr and Auburn) and they may have made other models as well. To date, no other models have turned up with Seiberling markings and no Seiberling catalogs have surfaced.

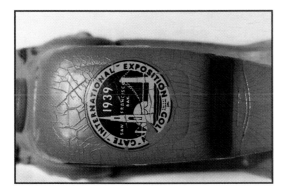

Golden Gate Ford
Photo courtesy of Carl Natter

We all know that Firestone made and sold Mercury toy automobiles at the Golden Gate International Exposition in San Francisco in 1939. Recently, we learned that Seiberling promoted their large 1935 Ford (GA01) at the Exposition, as well. Two examples are shown on this page, thanks to Carl Natter and Dick Ford.

I have observed that the small Fords come in many bright colors, as most rubber toys did, while the large Ford is found in colors that more nearly match those of the automobile itself, such as tan, gray, or dark red.

GA01
1935 Ford
two-door slantback sedan,
5".
$60.00 – 80.00.
Photo courtesy of Gates & Evelyn Willard

GA02
Two-door slantback sedan,
4".
$35.00 – 70.00.

GA01 (top)
1935 Ford
two-door slantback sedan,
5".
GA02 (bottom)
1935 Ford
two-door slantback sedan,
4".

THE PERFECT RUBBER COMPANY

In 1935, Pontiac introduced the famous Silver Streak, that was to become their most prominent styling feature for the next 20 years.

The Perfect Rubber Company of Mansfield, Ohio, made a well-detailed replica of the 1935 Pontiac slant-back sedan and sold the Pontiac Motor Company on the idea of using the small rubber toy as a promotional. Pontiac mailed a sample of the toy to each dealer and encouraged them to order directly from Perfect.

The small Pontiacs sold for nine cents each, when purchased by the gross, and for an extra two cents each, the dealer could have his name imprinted on the top. Dealers were urged to give these small Pontiacs to prospective buyers who came in to look at the new Silver Streak.

PA01
1935 Pontiac
slantback sedan,
3⅞".
$45.00 – 90.00.
Photo courtesy of Gates & Eve Willard

Charlie Sapp, who lives in Mt Vernon, Ohio, loaned me this terrific yellow Pontiac to photograph. This little car still resides in the original box that was mailed to Sapp Brothers in 1935, and includes the order blank one could use to order from Perfect.

1935 Pontiac in the original box mailed from Pontiac, Michigan. Note that a small package could be mailed for three cents.

Charlie's family had been in the automobile business since 1910 when they started Sapp Brothers as a Buick agency. In the late 20s, they added Cadillac and LaSalle to their line and eventually added Pontiac in 1932. Charlie worked there from 1938 until 1941, when he was drafted into the army.

Charlie said 1935 was a big year for Pontiac, as they shared a new streamlined, all-steel body with Chevrolet and Oldsmobile. He said that this four-door sedan sold for $865 in 1935, which is not much more than a tuneup these days.

Pontiac made very few changes in 1936 but they did drop the "suicide doors," which were hinged in the center post. The placement of the door handles on the Perfect 1936 Pontiac is the only difference I can see.

PA02
1936 Pontiac
slantback sedan,
$3\frac{7}{8}$".
$45.00 – 90.00.
Photo courtesy of Steve Butler

1936 Pontiac promotionals from
"Livermon Motor Co. Inc." in red.

1936 Pontiac promotionals from
"Livermon Motor Co. Inc." in
gray.
Photo courtesy of Steve Butler

PRICES

All shipments made in five bright assorted colors.

5 Assorted Colors

3 dozen (36)	$ 5.00
6 dozen (72)	7.20
12 dozen (144)	13.50
24 dozen (288)	23.50

Imprinted on top with your name and address.

3 dozen (36)	$1.50 extra
6 dozen (72)	2.00 extra
12 dozen (144)	2.50 extra
24 dozen (288)	3.75 extra

F. O. B. Mansfield, Ohio

TERMS

Cash with order or 50% with order. Balance C. O. D.

USE THIS ORDER BLANK

Date_____

THE PERFECT RUBBER COMPANY

Mansfield, Ohio

Gentlemen:

Ship at once_____Pontiac Miniature Rubber Sedans.

Check enclosed $_____

SHIP TO

Name_____

City_____ State____

If imprinted, type copy here:

_____

_____

_____

Signed :_____

Order blank for
1935 Perfect Pontiacs.

Sapp Brothers, Mt. Vernon,
Ohio, 1943.

Sapp Brothers ad in
the Knox County, Ohio,
Directory from 1937 – 39.

SAPP BROS. & CO.

Dealers

BUICK —— PONTIAC

Headquarters For

Reconditioned & Guaranteed

USED CARS

Pharis Tires — Delco Batteries

Phone 78   12 W. Ohio Ave.,
Mt. Vernon, Ohio

After this book was in final form, I obtained significant new information that I want to share. On the next page you will find an advertisement from the Perfect Rubber Company offering 1935 Dodge cars and trucks to dealers. Both of these vehicles are classified as "unknown" in a later section of the book. Now, I am satisfied that all of the 1935, 1936, and 1937 Dodge and Plymouth promotionals were made by Perfect. It is possible that the Chrysler and DeSoto airflows are also Perfect, but I am not prepared to go that far without additional evidence. Therefore, new Perfect designations are as follows:

PA01 – 1935 Pontiac
PA02 – 1936 Pontiac
PA03 – 1935 Plymouth
PA04 – 1936 Plymouth

PA05 – 1937 Plymouth
PA06 – 1935 Dodge
PT01 – 1935 Dodge truck

DODGE MINIATURE SEDANS and TRUCKS

(MOLDED RUBBER TOYS)

Furnished in Red, Yellow, Blue and Green.

Either with or without name neatly imprinted on top.

Order a supply today.

ACTUAL SIZE

Furnished in Yellow and Red.

Either with or without name neatly imprinted in bottom of truck body.

Order a supply today.

ACTUAL SIZE

A Proven Sales Help

PRICES

All Dodge Sedan shipments made in four assorted colors. Dodge Truck shipments made in Red and Yellow.

Quantity	
50	$ 7.50
100	13.00
250	30.00

IMPRINTED

Additional Charge for imprinting these cars with your name and address.

50-100	$1.50
250	2.50
500	3.50
1000	5.00

TERMS

Cash with order or 50% with order. Balance C. O. D. F. O. B. Mansfield, Ohio.

SUGGESTED USES FOR DODGE MINIATURE RUBBER TOYS

1. Canvass your owner list and give one with your compliments to each family that has a child.

2. Use a spot announcement on your local radio station featuring this new toy and fill your showroom with buyers.

3. Use them as souvenirs—place the mat plates at luncheons or banquets.

4. Run a small teaser ad in your local paper—advertise them as made entirely of rubber—harmless to woodwork or furniture—choice of four colors—paint non-poisonous.

IMPRINTED

Secure a quantity imprinted with your name and address for use at Christmas time. They will build for you *Good Will*, *public respect* and *appreciation*.

DODGE BROTHERS CORPORATION

USE THIS ORDER BLANK

THE PERFECT RUBBER COMPANY
MANSFIELD, OHIO

Check _____ Date _____
Dodge Sedan Models.

Gentlemen: Ship at once _____ Dodge Truck Models. Check enclosed $ _____
SHIP TO   If imprinted, type copy here:

Name _____

TOYCO

In our earlier book, we featured a small, solid rubber fastback sedan and two small, solid rubber, open-cockpit racers that were all classified as manufacturer unknown. Later, thanks to Charley Maledon, we learned that the little fastback was a TOYCO, as evidenced by this example with a small decal, which reads, "TOYCO Solid Rubber Toy." Several years later, I received a photo of the small racer, with an identical decal, from Pim Piet, from Holland. The larger racer has not turned up with a TOYCO decal but the design is so similar, we must conclude that it fits with the other two toys. Our knowledge of the history of these old toys is measured in very small steps.

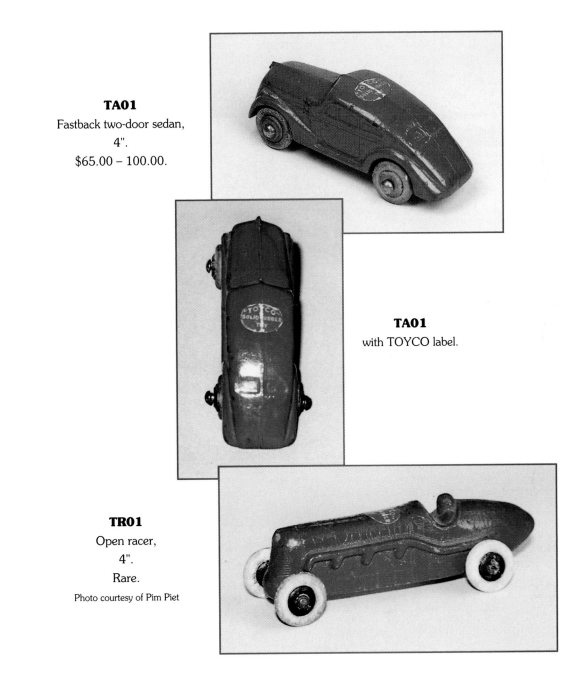

TA01
Fastback two-door sedan,
4".
$65.00 – 100.00.

TA01
with TOYCO label.

TR01
Open racer,
4".
Rare.
Photo courtesy of Pim Piet

TR01 (bottom)
TR02 (top)
5".
Rare.

TR02
Rare.
Photo courtesy of Ron Snow

TR03
Open racer,
5".
Rare.
Photo courtesy of Ron Snow

TR02, TR03
Focusing on differences in grill.
Photo courtesy of Ron Snow

THE 1935 FORD MYSTERY

The '35 Ford was a neat little car and provided a worthy prototype for many toy cars. The '35 Ford was by far the most popular model for rubber toys. In fact, it is the only model for all of the toys made by two manufacturers.

When I first began my research into early rubber toys, I was bewildered by the seemingly countless varieties and manufacturers of '35 Ford models. After much study, I still face a mystery concerning these little rubber cars.

Let's focus on the small Fords — approximately four inches in length. Both Firestone and Seiberling made a larger '35 Ford, which we address elsewhere. The four inch Fords came in five basic body styles: a three-window coupe, a slantback sedan, an ambulance (or panel truck), a stake body truck, and an army truck covered with canvas. We do not consider the panel truck and ambulance to be different models since the only difference is paint.

The small Fords were made by three companies for sure: the Auburn Rubber Company of Auburn, Indiana; The Barr Rubber Products Company of Sandusky, Ohio; and the Seiberling Latex Products Company of Akron, Ohio. There are also a number of rubber Fords that cannot be positively identified as the products of any of these three companies.

All of the small Fords appear to be identical from the outside. I can find no differences at all in the toys made by Auburn, Barr, or Seiberling. If you flip them over, they do have some obvious differences. The photo compares a Seiberling, an Auburn, a Barr, and an unmarked toy. The Auburn toy has a larger cavity and the axles are the type that penetrate completely through the toy and are visible in the middle of the underside. The Barr has a similar cavity but has nail-type axles, the tips of which can be seen in the center of the car. The Seiberling toys have smaller cavities and the axles (nail-type) sink into the solid body of the car and do not show at all. The unknown toy is designed exactly like the Seiberling, except it has no printing underneath, other than a mold number.

The accompanying chart provides a summary of the facts and uncertainties associated with the '35 Fords:

1. According to old Auburn advertising, they made a coupe, slantback, and stake body truck. I have never actually seen a stake truck marked "Auburn."

2. Barr had a 1935 advertisement which identified "Four Varieties" of Fords — a coupe, a slantback, a panel truck, and a stake truck. I have seen both sedans and coupes marked "Barr" but have never seen any variety of truck marked in this way.

3. Apparently, Seiberling made the slantback sedan and no other model. These toys are well marked underneath and include the name "Ford," in addition to company identification.

4. I have seen unmarked cars — both coupes and sedans, that would appear to be Auburn toys, based on the design of the mold cavity and the axles.

5. I have seen all five unmarked varieties that have the same basic design as the Seiberling.

The bottom line is that three companies made (and marked) small rubber Fords and perhaps other companies (that remain anonymous), made them as well. An easier explanation is that they were all made by these three companies, but some of them were unmarked, for reasons unknown. In any case, I think all of the molds were made by the same company or were blatantly copied by competitors.

I have no definite proof, but I think the ambulance version of the panel truck and the army version of the stake truck were both afterthoughts by Barr and were made exclusively by them.

Manufacturer	Coupe	Slantback	Ambulance/Panel	Stake Truck	Army Truck
Auburn	X	X		X	
Barr	X	X	X	X	
Seiberling		X			
Unmarked (like Auburn)	X	X			
Unmarked (like Seiberling)	X	X	X	X	X

Comparison of the mold cavities of four different 1935 Fords, left to right: Auburn, Barr, Seiberling, unknown.

OTHER PRE-WAR MYSTERIES

To this point, we have confidently cataloged many rubber toys, by manufacturer. The greatest number of early rubber toy vehicles were manufactured by the Auburn Rubber Company. The Sun Rubber Company was the second-largest producer of early rubber toys. Five other manufacturers — Barr, Rainbow, Firestone, Seiberling, and Perfect created very few varieties, compared to Auburn and Sun, but the ones they gave us are outstanding. Toyco made a fastback car and three racers of which we are aware.

UA01
1934 DeSoto Airflow
four-door sedan,
5".
$75.00 – 125.00.

We discussed the difficult task of cataloging the small 1935 Fords, by manufacturer, but we are confident that they were produced by either Auburn, Barr, or Seiberling.

A number of pre-war rubber toys exist, however, whose manufacturer remains a total mystery, and we have few clues upon which to venture even an educated guess.

The largest group of these unknowns are Chrysler Corporation promotionals used by local automobile dealers to promote the sale of their cars and trucks. Some of these promotionals are similar in their design but others are strikingly different. These toys probably represent the work of at least two manufacturers.

The DeSoto Airflow with Goodyear tires.
Was it a promotional for Goodyear?
Photo courtesy of Dick Ford

The promotionals are often found with dealerships identified by either ink stamps or decals on the toy itself. Others were never identified with a specific dealership and at least one of these — the 1934 Chrysler Airflow — was also sold in dime stores. The toy appeared in a 1935 Butler Brothers Wholesale catalog, wrapped in cellophane, but the manufacturer was not identified.

UA01

As a Black & White taxi promotional.

Photo courtesy of Dick Ford

UA02

1934 Chrysler Airflow,
two-door sedan,
5⅛".
$75.00 – 125.00.

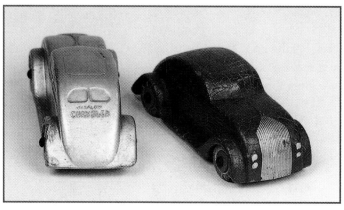

A Chrysler promotional from
"C. J. Zwoyer Maxatawny, Pa."
Dick Ford tells me that this old
dealership building is still there
in Maxatawny on Route 222,
between Reading and Allentown.

Another Dick Ford Chrysler promotional
this one from DuLaney-Miller.

Chrysler underside. This must have been a big concern for mothers in the thirties, because several companies that made rubber toys used the same type of advertising.

Photo courtesy of Bill Ferretti

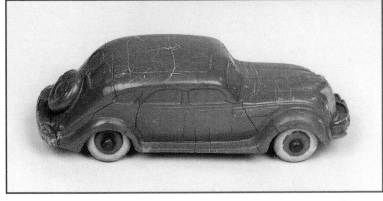

UA03
1935 Chrysler Airflow,
four-door sedan,
4¾".
Very rare.

Photo courtesy of Nelson Adams

UA04
1935 Plymouth
four-door sedan,
4⅞".
$90.00 – 200.00.

Photo courtesy of Dick Ford

UA05
1936 Plymouth
four-door sedan,
4⅞".
$90.00 – 200.00.

1936 Plymouth from "Truman
Bowen Co. Inc, Fort Peck, Mont."
Photo courtesy of Dick Ford

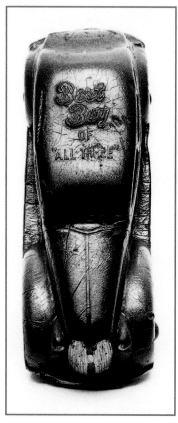

UA06
1937 Plymouth
four-door sedan,
4⅞".
$90.00 – 200.00.

1935, 1936, 1937 Plymouths.

Photo courtesy of Dick Ford

UA09
1935 Dodge sedan,
4⅞".
$150.00 – 250.00.

Dodge and Plymouth rear view.

Photo courtesy of Dick Ford

UA08
1942 Nash(?)
two-door sedan,
4".
$15.00 – 25.00.

UT01
1935 Dodge
rack truck,
4⅞".
Very rare.

From the Nelson Adams collection.

UT02
Tow truck (Pierce-Arrow?),
5¼".
Very rare.

Photo courtesy of Charley Maledon

Tow truck, rear view.

JUDY TOYS

The Judy Company, of Minneapolis, marketed "educational play material," according to their own advertising. One of their products was a hard rubber farm set, called Happy's Farm Family. The box is marked "copyright 1945," which means it probably sold into the early fifties, at which time it would have been competing with less expensive hard plastic and vinyl sets.

Happy's family includes a farmer (presumably Happy!), his wife, a boy, a girl, and a number of farm animals and fowl. Most importantly, as far as we are concerned, the set includes a car, a pickup truck, and a farm tractor with a driver (do you suppose the tractor driver could be "Happy," or is he just a hired hand?).

The people and animal figures are rather well designed and are three-dimensional. The vehicles, on the other hand, are essentially two-dimensional, being only wide enough to stand alone but not nearly as wide as they should be for realism. Collectors usually refer to toys such as these as "flat."

Happy's Farm Family boxed set.

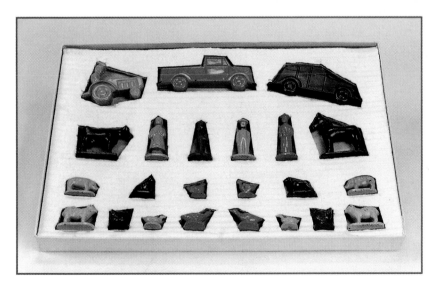

JA01
Sedan,
fastback, flat,
5¼".
$15.00 – 25.00.
JT01
Pickup truck,
flat,
5¼".
$15.00 – 25.00.
JF01
Farm tractor,
flat,
3½".
$15.00 – 25.00.

GIFT CRAFT

Gift Craft, a specialty company, operating out of Chicago, offered toys and games during the early post-war period. A February 1946 ad in *Playthings* magazine boasted prompt delivery of rubber toy automobiles and other products. Toy manufacturers, like most American industries were overwhelmed with orders for toys, following the close of the war. Most big companies, like Auburn and Sun, were heavily engaged in defense production and had difficulty gearing up for toy production quickly enough to meet the tremendous demand. This situation made it possible for a small company to step in and take a share of the market.

We do not know who actually manufactured these toy cars. Chances are, Gift Craft contracted with a small rubber manufacturing company to produce the toys and they handled the sales and distribution. Only one vehicle has been identified as a Gift Craft.

TA01
1946 Nash(?)
two-door
fastback sedan,
4".
$20.00 – 30.00.

GLOLITE

When *Rubber Toy Vehicles* was first published in 1994, we knew very little about Glolite. We knew they made a red crawler tractor that pulled a wooden trailer filled with lumber and the same tractor, in olive green, that pulled a 155mm Howitzer. Neither of these tractors had a driver nor a steering wheel. The name "Glolite" seemed strange for a toy that had no lights.

Tom Bishop, of Austin, Texas, knew even less about these toys at the time, but now he is my Glolite expert. Tom had bought a copy of *Rubber Toy Vehicles*, and was leafing through it, when the Glolite photo caught his eye. He knew he had seen that tractor before at a local antique store and rushed down to see if it was still there. It was, and soon became Tom's first Glolite toy. Tom stopped off to see a friend, who also ran an antique store, to show him his new prize. To Tom's amazement, his friend produced yet another Glolite from underneath the counter (this one in the original box with a driver included), which soon became Tom's second Glolite toy in one day. Since then, he has also obtained a Glolite Jeep and some catalogs, which he has shared with us. Now, due in large part to Tom's tenacity and research, we know a lot more about this obscure toy.

Glolite toys were made by the Glolite Corporation at 526 South Canal Street in Chicago, a division of Noma, known primarily as a maker of Christmas tree lights. Noma also made some toys from wood and composition materials (see catalogs), and marketed them under its own name. Tree lights were also packaged under the name Glolite, and toys in this line carried the same name. This is confusing, but at least we know where the name Glolite came from.

The crawler tractor has a water-slide decal, which bears the name Glolite. They were packaged and sold separately, as well as with other toys they pulled. The tractor is equipped with a metal blade up front in its civilian version. The driver is molded separately and has a steering wheel attached to his hands (which explains why the tractor has no steering wheel). Some are equipped with a clicker, which makes a sound as the toy is pulled. The military tractor has no blade, nor any holes where one could be mounted. This version does not have an exhaust stack nor a clicker.

The Glolite Jeep does not have a Glolite decal, but has a similar decal that serves as the front end detail, including the grill and headlights. The Jeep has a different, but similar, driver, and was sold with a utility trailer made of wood.

I have only seen the farm tractor and Jeep in red, although the catalog says the tractor is painted in "bright colors of red and green." The Jeep description simply says "finished in attractive colors." In advertisements, Glolite toys are said to be made of "Duro-Plastic" but a close look reveals that the black material has a rubber look and is probably a composition which contains rubber.

Glolite toys appeared in the 1945 Sears Christmas Catalog (catalogs) and the 1946 Jim Brown Catalog (catalogs). Perhaps the life of these toys was restricted to those two years.

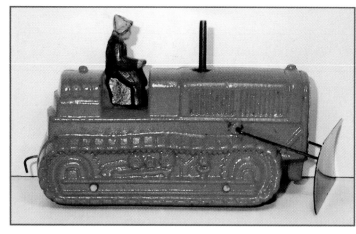

EF01
Crawler tractor,
9".
including blade.
$75.00 – 150.00.
Photo courtesy of Tom Bishop

EF01
Glolite decal.
Photo courtesy of Tom Bishop

Original box for EF01.
Photo courtesy of Tom Bishop

EF02
Crawler tractor,
with blade and ratchet (clicker).
Note description on box.
$75.00 – 150.00.
Photo courtesy of Charley Maledon

EF03
Crawler tractor/lumber trailer,
approx. 15".
Very rare.
Photo courtesy of Berni Carlson

EF04
Farm Jeep,
7".
Rare.
Photo courtesy of Tom Bishop

EF04
With driver in place.
Photo courtesy of Tom Bishop

EM01
Crawler tractor
with 155MM Howitzer,
23½".
Very rare.

Drivers for EF01 and EM01.

Photo courtesy of Bill Ferrretti

Drivers, rear view.

Photo courtesy of Bill Ferretti

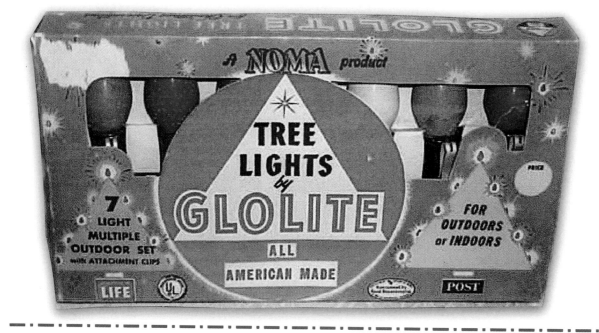

Glolite Christmas
tree lights.

VICEROY

The Viceroy Manufacturing Company, Limited, with locations in Toronto, Montreal, Winnepeg, and Vancouver, specialized in rubber and vinyl toys and dolls. They worked out some special arrangement with The Sun Rubber Company to manufacture and market certain Sun toys, which they added to their own line of distinctive Viceroy toys. This arrangement was apparently more than a simple case of borrowing the molds, because the Viceroy catalog and the toys themselves bear the "Sunruco" (Sun Rubber Company) trademark, along with their own.

The Viceroy versions of the Sun toys were painted in brighter colors and had much better detailed trim painting than the originals. The Viceroy "Super Racer" is even more distinctive because they added vertical stripes to the racer's design and fitted them with black tires, rather than the white ones used by Sun. The smaller racer appears to be an original Viceroy design.

VR01
Open racer,
Sun Rubber type,
6½".
$50.00 – 70.00.

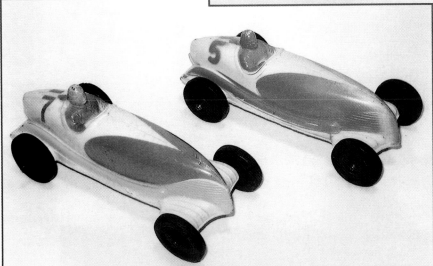

VR02
Open racer,
4½".
$40.00 – 60.00.

VD01
Mickey Mouse fire truck,
6¾".
$65.00 – 125.00.
Photo courtesy of Ron Snow

Mickey Mouse fire truck
Viceroy rubber (left),
Viceroy vinyl (center), and
Sun Rubber (right).
Photo courtesy of Bill Ferretti

VD02
Donald Duck roadster,
6⅝".
$65.00 – 125.00.
Photo courtesy Ron Snow

Viceroy Donald Duck roadster in rubber (left)
and vinyl (right).
Photo courtesy of Bill Feretti

The vinyl version is fitted
with a friction motor.
Photo courtesy of Bill Feretti

VD03
Mickey Mouse airplane,
6¼".
$65.00 – 125.00.
Photo courtesy of Bill Ferretti

VD04
Donald Duck airplane,
6¼".
$65.00 – 125.00.
Photo courtesy of Bill Ferretti

VD05
Mickey Mouse tractor,
4¾".
$65.00 – 125.00.
Photo courtesy of Ron Snow

VD06
Donald Duck tractor,
4¾".
$65.00 – 125.00.
Photo courtesy of Ron Snow

VICEROY VINYL

Like Auburn and Sun, Viceroy made a transition from rubber to vinyl and produced some very interesting toys along the way. The Donald Duck tractor was cast in vinyl in a one-wheel version, which sometimes included a friction motor. After dropping the Disney toys, they continued to produce toys in vinyl, as represented by these examples.

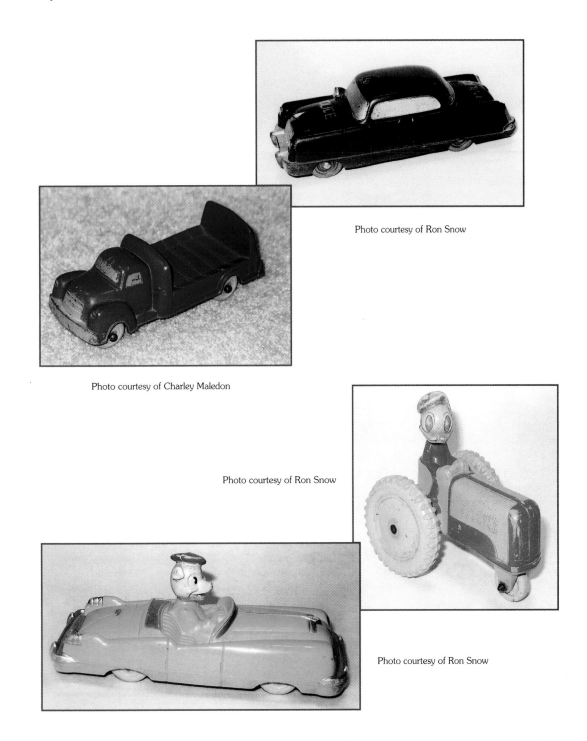

Photo courtesy of Ron Snow

Photo courtesy of Charley Maledon

Photo courtesy of Ron Snow

Photo courtesy of Ron Snow

TRUCKERS MARBLE COASTER

The Truckers Marble Coaster is not a rubber toy, per se, but incorporates an Auburn Rubber truck in its design.

The toy consists of three components:

1. A steel structure, 8 inches high and 10 inches long, composed of five ramps, which they call a "coaster."
2. An Auburn Rubber open truck.
3. A package of 26 marbles.

The design allows the marbles to be placed in the top ramp, where they roll down through the series of ramps and eventually into the truck bed. The bottom ramp has a weighted "stop" that prevents the marbles from rolling out until the weight is pushed back by the truck.

The toy was distributed by the C.W.M. Company of Cleveland, Ohio, during the early fifties. They may have manufactured the coaster structure itself but purchased the truck from Auburn and the marbles from a company who manufactured them.

The truck depicted on the box illustration is an AT09, 4⅛ inches long, but the truck that actually came in the package is an AT08, which is 5½ inches long. Chances are the smaller truck was never sold with the toy set because you can see in the illustration that the truck is already full of marbles and there are ten more rolling down the ramp. They probably realized that they would have to switch to a larger truck or cut back on the number of marbles. I have seen several of these toys and they always had the larger truck included.

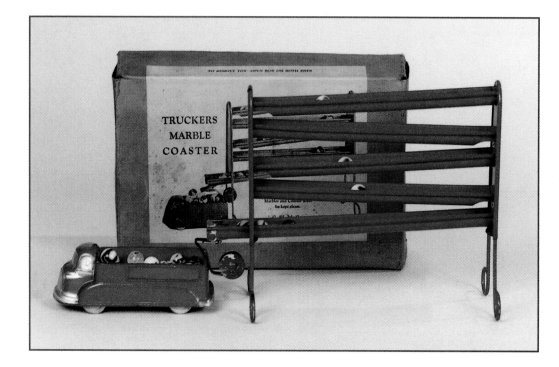

Truckers Marble Coaster.

RUBBER TOYS UNIQUE

Mr. F. H. Thurman worked for the Auburn Rubber Company as a toy designer for several years before the company closed down in Auburn, Indiana, and moved to Deming, New Mexico. When Mr. Thurman left Auburn, he started his own rubber design and production company, which he called Garrett Sales Corp. (because it was located in Garrett, Indiana) and later Rubber Toys Unique, Inc. Mr. Thurman was under restriction not to compete with Auburn in the manufacture of toys, so he concentrated on rubber mechanical products. When Auburn closed down for good in 1969, Mr. Thurman was free to get into the toy business himself.

Mr. Thurman designed and produced at least 18 different rubber vehicles. This sales brochure illustrates 14 varieties but he later added a "peanut car" in honor of President Carter, a "jelly bean car" for President Reagan, an elephant car, and a donkey car.

These toys were well made of heavy rubber and incorporated several technical improvements over the old hard rubber toys of the 1930s – 1950s. Mr. Thurman incorporates the color in the mixture itself, so that the toys do not have to be painted except for the silver trim. He also added an inhibitor to the material to prevent the hardening of the rubber over time.

A promotional ashtray, made of rubber, by Rubber Toys Unique.

Rubber Toys Unique (formerly called Garrett Sales Corp.) display.

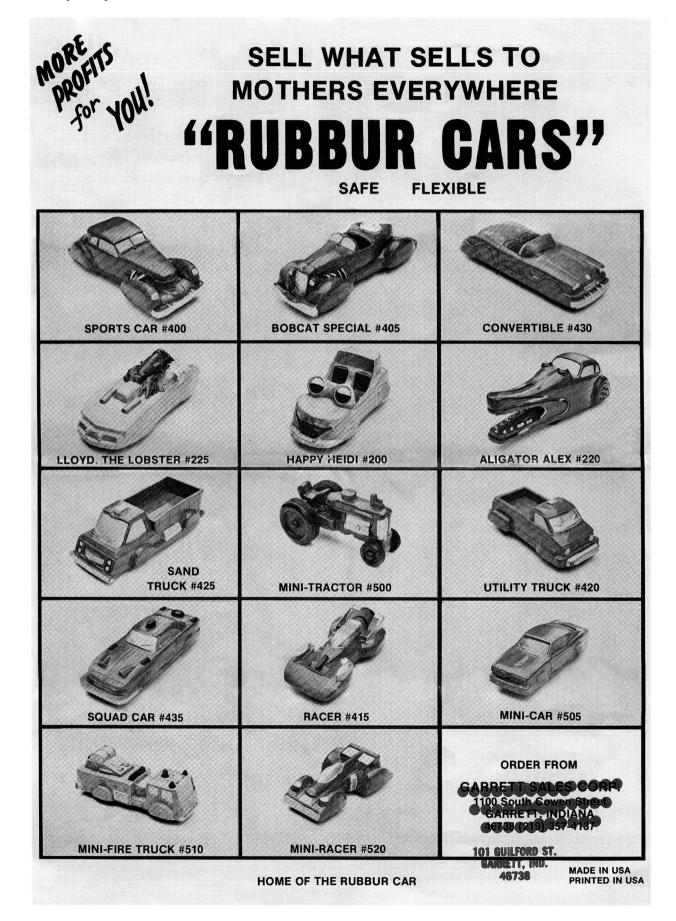

MORE PROFITS for YOU!

SELL WHAT SELLS TO MOTHERS EVERYWHERE
"RUBBUR CARS"
SAFE   FLEXIBLE

SPORTS CAR #400

BOBCAT SPECIAL #405

CONVERTIBLE #430

LLOYD, THE LOBSTER #225

HAPPY HEIDI #200

ALIGATOR ALEX #220

SAND TRUCK #425

MINI-TRACTOR #500

UTILITY TRUCK #420

SQUAD CAR #435

RACER #415

MINI-CAR #505

MINI-FIRE TRUCK #510

MINI-RACER #520

ORDER FROM

GARRETT SALES CORP.
1100 South Cowen Street
GARRETT, INDIANA
46738 (219) 357-4137

101 GUILFORD ST.
GARRETT, IND.
46738

MADE IN USA
PRINTED IN USA

HOME OF THE RUBBUR CAR

110

EMPIRE

We know little about the Empire Rubber Company of Dunstable, Bedford-shire, England. Since we originally researched rubber toy manufacturers, four previously unidentified toys have been identified as Empire toys.

According to my English friends, Empire manufactured rubber toys during the immediate postwar period (1946 – 51) and may have patterned some of them after American toys from the prewar era.

MA01
1935 Ford
slantback sedan,
5 ".

The 1935 Ford two-door slantback sedan is a pretty good depiction of a real 1935 Ford, but the hump in the back sets it apart from its American cousins. Fords built for the British market (Great Britain, Canada, Australia) were often offered in designs not available to American car buyers. It makes sense that the same would apply to toy Fords.

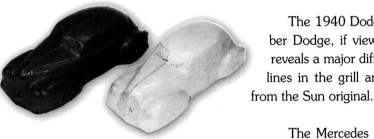

The 1940 Dodge sedan is the spitting image of a Sun Rubber Dodge, if viewed from certain angles. The head-on view reveals a major difference in the design of the grill. The vertical lines in the grill and headlights set the English version apart from the Sun original.

The Mercedes racer was previously classified as American-made but manufacturer unknown. This little solid-rubber racer has now been positively identified as Empire.

MA02
1940 Dodge sedan,
4½"
(blue car on the left),
MA03 (white car) is the same car with variations.
Note differences in grill and windshield wipers.
Photo courtesy of Bill Ferretti

MR01
Mercedes racer,
3½".

Empire Dodges, compared to the Sun model.
Photo courtesy of Bill Ferretti

DURAVIT

Years ago, I was approached by someone at a toy show who knew that I collected rubber toys. He presented me with a huge Ford pickup, which turned out to be a Duravit, made in Argentina. That was the extent of my knowledge about Duravit toys until fairly recently when the Internet has made these toys available to the American market.

Duravits are heavy, well-made toys, based on real American or European vehicles. Most are from the 1960 – 1980 era. In size, they compare more to Tonka and Buddy L than to other rubber toys, which puts them in a class by themselves.

Bill Ferretti, who lives near Atlanta, collects Duravits with a passion. Thanks to Bill, we have this beautiful gallery of his toys.

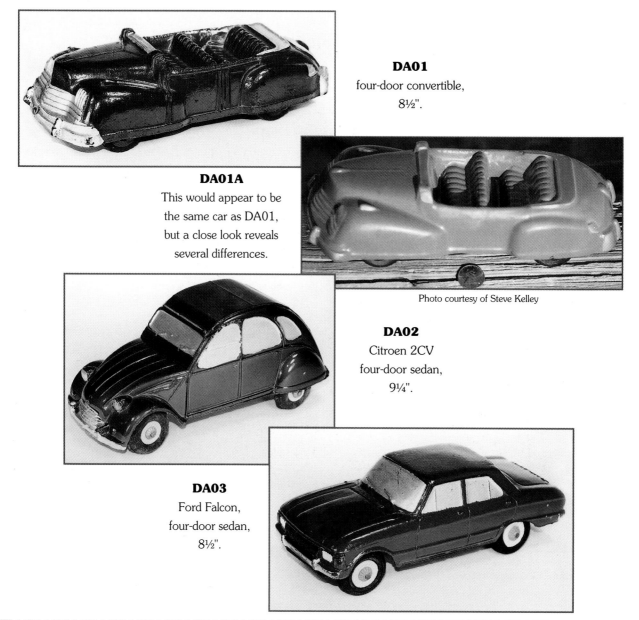

DA01
four-door convertible,
8½".

DA01A
This would appear to be
the same car as DA01,
but a close look reveals
several differences.

Photo courtesy of Steve Kelley

DA02
Citroen 2CV
four-door sedan,
9¼".

DA03
Ford Falcon,
four-door sedan,
8½".

DA04
Ford Falcon
station wagon,
10".

DA05
Fiat 500
two-door sedan,
7½".

DA06
Peugeot 504
four-door sedan,
10½".

This is the way new Duravits are packaged.

DA07
Renault 12
station wagon,
10".

DA08
Ford Group
6 racer,
8".

DA09
Sports car (Datsun?),
9".

DA10
Jeep,
7".

DT01
1970 Ford
F 100 pickup,
17½".

DT02 (top),
Ford
F100 pickup,
18".

DT03 (bottom)
Ford
F100 pickup,
11¼".
Note that DT02 is similar
to DT01, but is slightly larger
and has "Duravit" on the front.

DT04
Mercedes-Benz 113
flat bed,
8".

DT05
Mercedes-Benz
tractor trailer (tanker),
22",
with original box.

DT05
Underside, which reveals hose used
for draining liquid from hollow tanker.
Sun Rubber teardrop sedan, at
5½",
puts this huge toy in perspective.

DT06
Tractor with open trailer,
17".

DT07
Flat bed dump (Ford?),
9".

DF01
Loader, metal bucket,
15¾".

OTHER FOREIGN TOYS

Citroen, Pneu Bata (Czechoslovakia),
5¼".

From the Dennis Dawson collection

Citroen, Pneu Bata (Czechoslovakia),
5¼".

From the Dennis Dawson collection

Tatraplan (Czechoslovakia),
with windup motor,
6½".

Tatraplan, rear view.

Steha,
early 1950s Volkswagon,
Germany,
10".

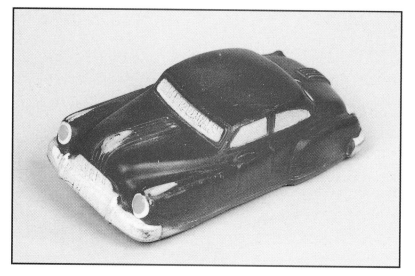

1950 Pontiac,
5½".
Japan.

Sarmi Donald Duck car (Australia),
6½".
This appears to be a knockoff of
the Sun Rubber toy. This one does not
have the Donald Duck printing on the side.
Photo courtesy of Bill Ferretti

Auto Union racer (Brazil),
7¼".
Photo courtesy of Bill Ferretti

Buick Fastback, c.1947,
9".
Bill Brisbane bought this
car when he was working
in Brazil. He was told the toy
originally came from South Africa.

SOLDIER SET #231

9 privates, 1 machine gunner, 2 charging soldiers, 1 bugler, 1 officer, 1 officer on horse.

FIRST AID SET #237

2 wounded soldiers, 2 signal men, doctor, 2 nurses, stretcher, 2 stretcher bearers, ambulance, doctor's car, motor cop.

WHEEL SET# 503

Large automobile and large truck, motorcycle cop, 3 small automobiles, 2 small trucks, truck with 6 milk cans, 2 barrels and 1 box.

1940 Auburn catalog

RACING SET #555

4 large racers, 4 midget racers, motorcycle cop.

•

FARM IMPLEMENT SET #505

Large truck, tractor, spreader, plow, thresher, seeder, disc and wagon.

•

TANK SET #507

3 tanks, motorcycle with side car, 2 trucks, 1 cannon, 1 U. S. Army automobile.

•

Illustrated on these pages are some of the sales aids that the Auburn Rubber Corporation is offering to progressive toy retailers to increase sales of toys made of rubber. You will want these new Auburn packages. They will make it easy for you to sell more toys. They will boost your sales, and build customer satisfaction.

1940 Auburn catalog

1556   1536   1532   1566

256   252   250   254   258   1558

232   204   200   238   222   234   202

ASSORTMENTS FOR STOCK CONVENIENCE

#2342A • 10c SOLDIER ITEMS consists of four each of the following items: #232, #242, #240 to a dozen container.

#2508A • BASEBALL ASSORTMENT consists of two #250, two #254, fourteen #256, four #258, two #252 to a 2-dozen container packed half grey, half white.

#2606A • FOOTBALL ASSORTMENT consists of one center #264, six linemen #260, three backfielders #262, one passer #266, one runner #268 to a 2-dozen container, packed half red, half blue.

#1226A • 5c WHEEL ASSORTMENT consists of 8 pieces each (assorted colors) racer #1566, truck #1532, Plymouth #1552 to a 2-dozen container.

#1846A • 10c WHEEL ASSORTMENT consists of 4 pieces each (assorted colors) automobile #1558, truck #1534, racer #1536 to a dozen container.

#1546 MOTORCYCLE COP 5" long, 3½" high. Red with black trim.

#1702 STRETCHER 5" long, 1½" wide. White.

#1532 SMALL STAKE TRUCK 4" long, 1½" high. Assorted. 6 red, 3 orange, 3 green.

#1536 LARGE RACER 6¾" long, 2¼" high. Assorted 6 red, 2 orange, 2 green, 2 blue to dozen.

#1556 LARGE 25c RACER 11¼" long, 3" high. Asstd. 6 red, 2 green, 2 blue, 2 orange to dozen.

#1566 SMALL RACER 5" long, 1½" high. Asstd. 6 red, 2 orange, 2 blue, 2 green to dozen.

#1558 LARGE SEDAN Modern styling, 6" long, 2" high. Asstd. 6 red, 2 orange, 2 blue, 2 green to dozen.

#250 PITCHER 3½" high. Gray uniform (250 W white uniform, blue stockings, and cap) red stockings and cap, black belt.

#252 BATTER 3½" high. Gray uniform (252 W white uniform, blue stockings and cap) red stockings and cap, black belt.

#254 CATCHER 2⅝" high. Gray uniform (254 W white uniform, blue stockings and cap) red stockings and cap, brown glove, chest protector and mask.

#256 FIELDER OR BASEMAN 3¼" high. Gray uniform (256 W white uniform, blue stockings and cap) red stockings, cap, black belt.

#258 BASERUNNER 3⅛" high. Gray uniform (258 W white uniform, blue stockings and cap) red stockings and cap, black belt.

#200 U. S. INFANTRY PRIVATE 3⅛" high. Khaki with black and yellow trim (210 B blue). Black gun, orange puttees, silver helmet.

#202 BUGLER U. S. INFANTRY 3⅛" high. Khaki with black and yellow trim (212 B blue). Orange puttees, silver bugle and helmet.

#204 U. S. INFANTRY OFFICER 3⅛" high. Khaki with brown and yellow trim (204 B blue).

#222 SNIPER Crawling position, 1" high, 3⅝" long. Khaki with black trim, orange puttees, silver helmet.

#232 OFFICER ON HORSE 4" high. Khaki with black, red and yellow trim.

#234 BOMB THROWER 3½" high. Khaki with black and yellow trim. Orange puttees, silver helmet.

#238 CHARGING SOLDIER 2¾" high. Khaki with black trim. Black gun, silver helmet, orange puttees.

1940 Auburn catalog

#509 STREAMLINE TRANSPORT TRUCK 12" long, 2¼" high. Blue truck unit with detachable red trailer with 2 small cars.

#1534 LARGE STAKE TRUCK 5½" long, 2½" wide, 2" high. Asstd. 6 red, 3 orange, 3 green to dozen.

#1552 SMALL SEDAN 4" long, 1½" high. Asstd. 6 red, 2 orange, 2 blue, 2 green to dozen.

#260 LINEMAN 2" high. Khaki trousers, red shirt (260 B blue shirt) white helmet, black shoes.

#262 BACKFIELDMAN 3" high. Khaki trousers, red shirt (262 B blue shirt) white helmet, black shoes.

#264 CENTER 2" high. Khaki trousers, red shirt (264 B blue shirt) white helmet, black shoes.

#266 PASSER 3¼" high. Khaki trousers, red shirt (266 B blue shirt) white helmet, black shoes.

#268 CARRIER 3" high. Khaki trousers, red shirt (268 B blue shirt) white helmet, black shoes.

#1580 ARMY TANK 4¾" long by 3¼" high. Khaki with black trim.

#216 OBSERVER WITH BINOCULARS 2½" high. Khaki with black and yellow trim. Silver helmet and lenses. Orange puttees.

#230 MACHINE GUNNER Crouching position 1¾" high, 2½" long. Khaki with black and yellow trim. Silver helmet.

#236 SIGNALMAN 4¼" high. Khaki with black and yellow trim. Orange puttees, silver helmet, red and white flag.

#240 MOTORCYCLE SOLDIERS 10c retail. 2¼" high, 3¼" long. Two soldiers in motorcycle with side car. Khaki with black trim, silver helmets.

#242 ANTI-AIRCRAFT GUN 4¼" high, 3" long. Khaki with black and silver trim. Orange puttees, silver helmet.

#206 STRETCHER BEARER 3" high. Khaki with brown and yellow trim. Orange puttees. Styled to carry standard stretcher.

#208 WOUNDED SOLDIER Prone figure 3¼" long. Khaki with black and yellow trim. Orange puttees. White bandages on arm, head, one leg.

#224 RED CROSS DOCTOR 3¼" high. White with black and red trim.

#226 RED CROSS NURSE 3⅛" high. White with black and red trim.

#544 ARMY TRUCK 5½" long, 2½" wide, 2" high. Khaki with U.S.A. lettering.

1940 Auburn catalog

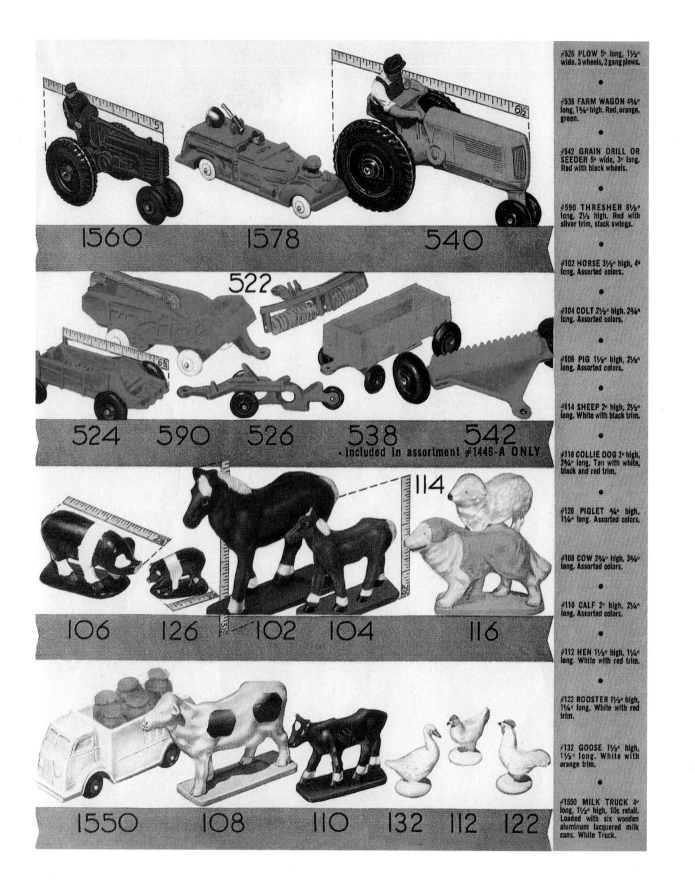

1560 1578 540

522

524 590 526 538 542

• included in assortment #1446-A ONLY

106 126 102 104 116

1550 108 110 132 112 122

#526 PLOW 5" long, 1½" wide. 3 wheels, 2 gang plows.

#538 FARM WAGON 4¾" long, 1¾" high. Red, orange, green.

#542 GRAIN DRILL OR SEEDER 5" wide, 3" long. Red with black wheels.

#590 THRESHER 6½" long, 2½ high. Red with silver trim, stack swings.

#102 HORSE 3½" high, 4" long. Assorted colors.

#104 COLT 2½" high, 2¾" long. Assorted colors.

#106 PIG 1½" high, 2½" long. Assorted colors.

#114 SHEEP 2" high, 2½" long. White with black trim.

#116 COLLIE DOG 2" high, 2¾" long. Tan with white, black and red trim.

#126 PIGLET ¾" high, 1¼" long. Assorted colors.

#108 COW 2¾" high, 3¾" long. Assorted colors.

#110 CALF 2" high, 2¼" long. Assorted colors.

#112 HEN 1½" high, 1¼" long. White with red trim.

#122 ROOSTER 1½" high, 1¼" long. White with red trim.

#132 GOOSE 1½" high, 1½" long. White with orange trim.

#1550 MILK TRUCK 4" long, 1½" high, 10c retail. Loaded with six wooden aluminum lacquered milk cans. White Truck.

1940 Auburn catalog

#586 ARMY PURSUIT PLANE 3½" long, 4¾" wing spread. Asstd. 6 red, 6 silver, to dozen.

#1548 AIRPLANE Replica Atlantic Clipper, 5½" long, 7¾" wing spread. Asstd. 6 red, 6 silver to dozen.

#1570 ENGINE AND TENDER 25c retail, 11" long, 2" high. Gray with black.

#1572 GONDOLA CAR 5½" long, 1½" high, 10c retail. Black truck with bed in asstd. colors, 8 red, 4 green to dozen.

#1574 DUMP CAR 10c retail, 5½" long, 1¾" high. Black trucks with swinging dump in asstd. colors. 6 red, 3 green, 3 orange to dz.

#1576 CABOOSE 10c retail. 4½" long, 2¼" high. Red body on black trucks.

#1582 BATTLESHIP 8¼" long by 2" high. Gray with black trim.

#540 LARGE OLIVER TRACTOR 25c retail, 6½" long, 4¼" high. Prominent driver decorated, black hat and shoes, white shirt, blue overalls, 6 red, 3 orange, 3 green to dozen.

#1560 JOHN DEERE TRACTOR 5" long, 3¾" high. Asstd. 6 red, 3 green, 3 orange to dozen.

#1578 FIRE ENGINE 5½" long by 2¼" high. Red with black trim.

#522 DISC HARROW 4¼" wide, 2½" long. Red.

#524 SPREADER 5" long, 2¼" wide. Red.

ASSORTMENTS FOR STOCK CONVENIENCE (Continued)

#1446A • FARM IMPLEMENT ASSORTMENT consists of 3 tractors #1560, 2 spreaders #524, 2 plows #526, 2 wagons #538, 1 seeder #542, 1 disc #522, 1 thresher #562 to a dozen container, one assortment only.

#1326A • 2 for 5c ANIMAL ASSORTMENT consists of 1 dozen each, rooster #122, hen #112, piglet #126, geese #132 to a 4-dozen container.

 # 200A • SOLDIER ASSORTMENT consists of 6 each of #200 and #238, 2 each of #202, #204, #234, #216, #230, #236 to a 2-dozen container.

#4046A • ASSORTED 5c ANIMALS consists of 4 colts, 6 calves, 6 sheep, 2 collies, 6 pigs to a 2-dozen container — assorted colors.

#1028A • ASSORTED 10c ANIMALS consists of 6 horses, 6 cows to a 1-dozen container — assorted colors.

1940 Auburn catalog

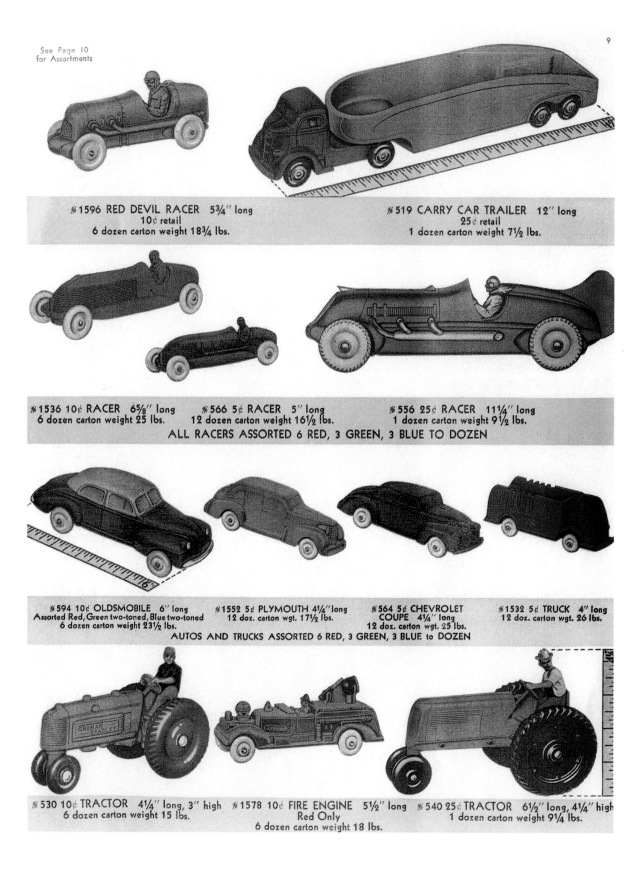

See Page 10
for Assortments

#1596 RED DEVIL RACER 5¾" long
10¢ retail
6 dozen carton weight 18¾ lbs.

#519 CARRY CAR TRAILER 12" long
25¢ retail
1 dozen carton weight 7½ lbs.

#1536 10¢ RACER 6⅝" long
6 dozen carton weight 25 lbs.

#566 5¢ RACER 5" long
12 dozen carton weight 16½ lbs.

#556 25¢ RACER 11¼" long
1 dozen carton weight 9½ lbs.

ALL RACERS ASSORTED 6 RED, 3 GREEN, 3 BLUE TO DOZEN

#594 10¢ OLDSMOBILE 6" long
Assorted Red, Green two-toned, Blue two-toned
6 dozen carton weight 23½ lbs.

#1552 5¢ PLYMOUTH 4¼" long
12 doz. carton wgt. 17½ lbs.

#564 5¢ CHEVROLET
COUPE 4¼" long
12 doz. carton wgt. 25 lbs.

#1532 5¢ TRUCK 4" long
12 doz. carton wgt. 26 lbs.

AUTOS AND TRUCKS ASSORTED 6 RED, 3 GREEN, 3 BLUE to DOZEN

#530 10¢ TRACTOR 4¼" long, 3" high
6 dozen carton weight 15 lbs.

#1578 10¢ FIRE ENGINE 5½" long
Red Only
6 dozen carton weight 18 lbs.

#540 25¢ TRACTOR 6½" long, 4¼" high
1 dozen carton weight 9¼ lbs.

1941 Auburn catalog

Courtesy Richard O'Brien

1941 Auburn catalog

Courtesy Richard O'Brien

The 1941 Auburn bulk line offers the most complete selection in the molded rubber toy field. Every item has been sales tested, that is, store tested for ability to sell. Every item has been verified for style and accuracy of detail. New numbers, particularly soldiers to meet the growing interest in military activities, have been added —thus making the Auburn line timely and profitable for all. Firms that have featured our complete bulk line have developed a remarkable year around volume.

BULK ASSORTMENTS

To meet the needs of the customer serving the smaller outlets, we have widened our range of assortments. There are now eleven selected assortments covering nearly every toy in the line in proved sales proportions.

See complete assortment descriptions on page 10.

PACKAGING

5¢ toys are packed 2 dozen to inside chipboard container, 12 dozen to corrugated shipping carton.

10¢ toys are packed 1 dozen to inside chipboard container, 6 dozen to corrugated shipping carton.

25¢ toys are packed 1 dozen to shipping carton.

See Page 10 for Assortments

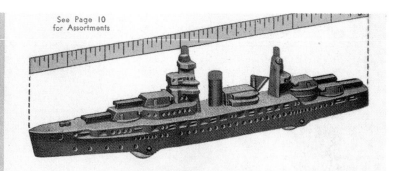

#1588 DREADNAUGHT 9⅛" long 10¢ retail
6 dozen shipping carton, weight 14 lbs.

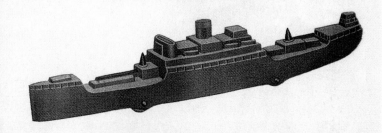

#1592 FREIGHTER 9¼" long 10¢ retail
6 dozen shipping carton, weight 14 lbs.

#582 BATTLESHIP 8¼" long 10¢ retail
6 dozen shipping carton, weight 13 lbs.

#1584 SUBMARINE
6¾" long 5¢ retail

#1534 TRUCK 5½" long 10¢ retail
Assorted 6 Red, 3 Green, 3 Blue to dozen

1941 Auburn catalog

Courtesy Richard O'Brien

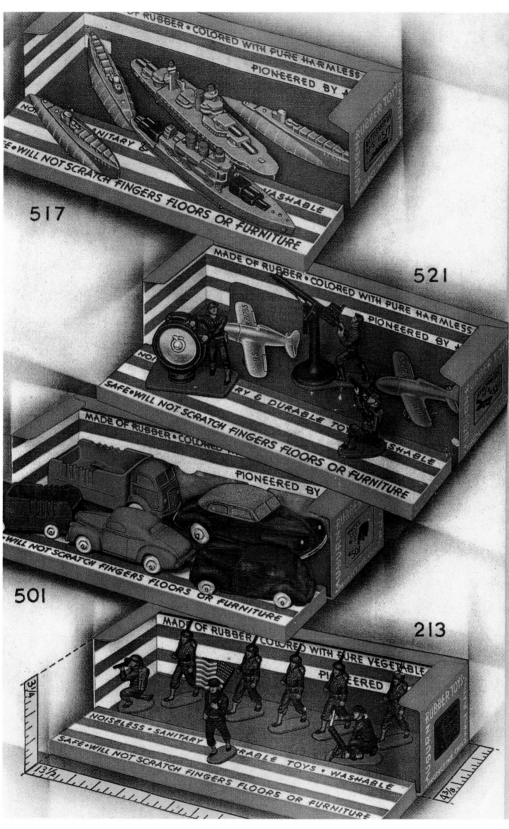

1941 Auburn catalog

Courtesy Richard O'Brien

BATTLESHI
SET #51

Battleship, dread
naught, 3 subma
rines. 50¢ retai

●

AVIATIO
SET #52

Search light, ai
craft defende
plane shooter,
airplanes. 50¢ re
tail.

●

WHEEL
SET # 50

Large truck, larg
automobile, sma
truck, small sedan
small coupe. 50
retail.

●

COLOR
GUARD
SET #2

Color bearer, trenc
mortar, 3 firing lir
soldiers, 3 march
ing soldiers. 50
retail.

●

50¢ sets packed
dozen to shippin
carton, average ca
ton weight 25 lb:

AUTOMOBILES AND AIRPLANES   Auburn Rubber Corp., Auburn, Indiana   Page 3

CUTS ARE FULL SIZE

Non pull out (patent pending) double head axles

No. 500 Cord Front Drive.
   Colors: red, green, silver.
   Asstd. 9 red, 2 green, 1 silver to dozen.

No. 504 Ford Coupe.
   Colors: red, green, silver.
   Asstd. 9 red, 2 green, 1 silver to dozen.

No. 502 Ford Sedan.
   Colors: red, green, silver.
   Asstd. 9 red, 2 green, 1 silver to dozen.

No. 506 Airplane (small): red and silver.
   Assorted 6 red, 6 silver to dozen.

No. 508 Airplane (large): black trim.
   Colored: red and silver.
   Assorted 6 red, 6 silver to dozen.

1936 Auburn catalog page

Courtesy Hope McCandlish Rider

1938 Auburn ad

Playthings

SUNRUCO
RUBBER PLAYTHINGS

1936

No. 1000 Racer
6½" Long
Shipping weight about 52 lbs. per gross.

No. 1005 Truck
Open body.
5¼" Long
Shipping weight about 50 lbs. per gross.

No. 1010 Sedan
5½" Long
Shipping weight about 46 lbs. per gross.

● COLOR ASSORTMENT:—ALL STYLES, 9 RED, 2 GREEN, 1 BLUE TO DOZEN.

● MINIMUM PACKING:—ALL STYLES, 3 DOZEN TO A SHIPPING CONTAINER.

No. 500 Sedan
4" Long
Shipping weight about 28 lbs. per gross.

No. 505 Racer
4⅜" Long
Shipping weight about 22 lbs. per gross.

No. 520 Bus
4¼" Long
Shipping weight about 28 lbs. per gross.

No. 510 Truck
Open body.
4¼" Long
Shipping weight about 30 lbs. per gross.

No. 515 Coupe
4" Long
Shipping weight about 26 lbs. per gross.

"SUNRUCO" RUBBER TOY AUTO AXLE ASSEMBLY
Patent No. 2,035,081

● One piece solid nickeled steel axle.
● Button hub cap prevents easy removal of wheel.
● All rubber wheel.
● Axle fits snugly in transverse groove through rubber body of toy, making true wheel alignment.
● "Sunruco" construction eliminates sharp pointed nails, that are easy to remove, and are a danger to children.

THE SUN RUBBER COMPANY, BARBERTON, OHIO, U. S. A.

1936 Sun Rubber catalog

Courtesy Howard Steinberg

No. 12011 Master Truck

No. 12015 Medium Tank

No. 12012 Super Racer

No. 12009 Transport

No. 12014 Army Scout Car

No. 12010 Dual-Control Plane

No. 12003 Truck

No. 12016 Teardrop Sedan

No. 13001 Sponge Rubber Blocks

1947 Sun Rubber catalog

Courtesy Bill Ferritti

No. 12008 Racing Plane

No. 12004 Coupe

No. 12002 Racer

No 12001 Sedan

No. 12006 Ambulance

No. 12013 Trailer Truck

No. 12005 Bus

No. 12007 Station Wagon

No. 12017 Fire Truck

Sunruco
RUBBER TOYS
ARE "TOPS" IN
EYE APPEAL AND
SALES APPEAL!

No. 12019
Mickey Mouse Aeroplane

No. 12018
Donald Duck Roadster

No. 12020
Mickey Mouse Tractor

© WALT DISNEY
PRODUCTIONS

THE SUN RUBBER COMPANY • BARBERTON, OHIO.

S 546-18

1948 Sun Rubber catalog

Courtesy Howard Steinberg

THESE POPULAR *Sunruco* RUBBER WHEEL TOY:

. . . realistically molded . . . sturdily built

No. 12001—Sedan, 4½ in. long. Packed 3 doz. in ctn. Weight, 7½ lbs.

No. 12002—Small Racer — 2 drivers, 4⅜ in. long. Packed 3 doz. in ctn. Weight, 6 lbs.

No. 12004—Coupe, 4 in. long. Packed 3 doz. in ctn. Weight, 6 lbs.

Order by Number

No. 12005—Passenger Bus, 4¼ in. long. Packed 3 doz. in ctn. Weight, 6½ lbs.

No. 12007—Station Wagon, 3¾ in. long. Packed 3 doz. in ctn. Weight, 6 lbs.

No. 12011—Two-Tone Master Truck, authentically designed, 6⅝ in. long. Packed 3 doz. in ctn. Weight, 16½ lbs.

No. 12012—Super Racer, 6¾ in. long. Plenty of flash in this racy miniature. Packed 3 doz. in ctn. Weight, 13 lbs.

1948 Sun Rubber catalog

Courtesy Howard Steinberg

RE PROVEN *Profit Makers!*

DISNEY WHEEL TOYS
by
Sunruco

© WDP

© WDP

No. 12017—Mickey Mouse Fire Truck, 6¾ in. long by 4 in. high. Packed 1 doz. in ctn. Weight, 8 lbs.

No. 12018—Donald Duck Roadster, 6-9/16 in. long by 3-13/16 in. high by 2-7/16 in. wide. Packed 1 doz. in ctn. asstd., 8 red, 4 yellow. Weight, 8 lbs.

they're flashy!
they're life-like!
they're low priced!

© WDP

© WDP

No. 12019—Mickey Mouse Aeroplane, 6¼ in. long by 3-7/16 in. high. Packed 1 doz. in ctn. asstd., 8 red, 4 blue. Weight 7 lbs.

No. 12020—Mickey Mouse Tractor, 4¾ in. long by 4-7/16 in. high. Packed 1 doz. in ctn. Weight, 7½ lbs.

Order by Number

© Copyright by Walt Disney Productions, Burbank, Calif.

Sunruco

1948 Sun Rubber catalog

Courtesy Howard Steinberg

TIMED FOR PEAK INTEREST
THE NEW *Sunruco* LINE OF

No. 12106—Army Ambulance, 3¾ in. long. Base color, army drab. Bumper, grille, cross insignia at top and two sides in silver. Rubber wheels, steel axles. Packed 3 doz. to ctn. Weight, 5¾ lbs.

No. 12108 — Scout Plane, 3 in. long, wing spread, 4⅛ in. Base color, army drab. Cockpit and insignia on wing in silver. Propeller revolves. Rubber wheels, steel axles. Packed 3 doz. to ctn. Weight, 3¾ lbs.

No. 12103 — Small Army Truck 4½ in. long, open body model. Base color, army drab. Bumper, grille, windows, and star on top of cab in silver. Rubber wheels, steel axles. Packed 3 doz. to a ctn. Weight 8 lbs.

 TOYS in tune with our Times

• AUTHENTICALLY MOLDED WHEEL TOY

No. 12114—Army Scout Car, 6¾ in. long. Base color army drab. Silver trim includes machine guns and radio. Bright red helmets of soldiers add a sparkling touch to this attractive miniature. Rubber wheels, steel axles. Packed doz. to a ctn. Weight, 9 lbs.

Order by

No. 12114
Army Scout Car

THE SUN RUBBER COMPANY

1948 Sun Rubber catalog

Courtesy Howard Steinberg

– AND HIGH VOLUME SALES...
U. S. ARMY MODEL RUBBER TOYS

No. 12109 – Transport Plane, 4 in. long, wing spread, 6 in. Base color, army drab. Cabin windows and insignia on right wing in silver. Four propellers revolve. Rubber wheels, steel axles and propeller shafts. Packed 3 doz. to a ctn. Weight, 7½ lbs.

No. 12111 – Large Army Truck, 5¾ in. long, open body model. Base color, army drab; grille, headlights, windows, lettering and star on top of cab in silver. Rubber wheels, steel axles. Packed 3 doz. to a ctn. Weight 16½ lbs.

INSPIRED BY U. S. ARMY MODELS •

SELL THE *Complete* ARMY LINE!

No. 12115 – Army Tank, 6 in. long. Base color, army drab. Revolving turret and gunner in brilliant canary yellow. Four gun mounts and guns in silver. Silver star and silver bogey wheels in relief. Bogey wheel hangers in cherry red complete the bright color scheme of this authentic miniature. Rubber running wheels, steel axles. Packed 1 doz. to a ctn. Weight, 9 lbs.

Number

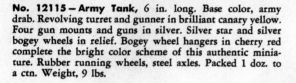

No. 12115
Army Tank

..... BARBERTON, OHIO .....

1948 Sun Rubber catalog

Courtesy Howard Steinberg

VICEROY safe, sturdy, moulded rubber wheel toys are realistic in appearance and all Disney character toys have movable heads. Colour decorations are applied after toys have been subjected to special process so that paint will not chip, crack or peel. Cannot damage furniture, floors or other surfaces.

No. 12017 "MICKEY MOUSE"© FIRE TRUCK. 6¾" long. Individual tissue wrap. 1 dozen to a shipping container. Approximate weight 7 lbs. per dozen.

No. 12018 "DONALD DUCK"© ROADSTER. 6⅝" long light blue with yellow trim or Bright red with yellow trim. Specify base colour desired when ordering. Individual tissue wrap. 1 dozen of a colour to a shipping container. Approximate weight 7 lbs. per dozen.

No. 12019 "MICKEY MOUSE"© AEROPLANE. 6¼ "long Yellow with red trim or bright green with yellow trim. Specify base colour desired when ordering. Individual tissue wrap. 1 dozen of a colour to a shipping container. Approximate weight 7½ lbs. per dozen.

No. 12013 "DONALD DUCK"© AEROPLANE. Same as No. 12019 but with Donald Duck head.

No. 12020 "MICKEY MOUSE"© TRACTOR. 4¾" long Yellow with dark blue trim or Red with silver trim. Specify base colour desired when ordering. Individual tissue wrap. 1 dozen of a colour to a shipping container. Approximate weight 7 lbs. per dozen.

No. 12028 "DONALD DUCK"© TRACTOR. Same as No. 12020 but with Donald Duck head.

No. 12012 SUPER RACER. 6¾" long. Red with white trim and yellow with dark blue trim. Individual tissue wrap. 2 dozen (assorted colour combinations) to a shipping container. Approximate weight 4½ lbs. per dozen.

No. 12010 JUNIOR RACER. 4½" long. Yellow with red trim and red with white trim. Individual tissue wrap. 3 dozen (assorted colour combinations) to a shipping container. Approximate weight 2¼ lbs. per dozen.

© W.D.P.—Walt Disney Productions

1951 Viceroy catalog

Courtesy Dennis Dawson

1945 Sears catalog

Courtesy Tom Bishop

For a happy playtime . . . fine Toys by NOMA, makers of famous NOMA Lights

A **Colorful Steam Shovel.** What fun your child will have with this interesting toy. He'll get such pleasure pretending to be an engineer building roads, dams, etc. . . . working the crane to dig grooves or lift loads. Skillfully made of red and gray painted wood . . . smoothly finished. Cab swings on swivel. Simple to raise and lower shovel by turning crank. Cab with shovel extended measures 9x5x15 inches. This fine toy will be a favorite of any active child.
49 N 5454—Shipping weight, 1 pound. .$1.73 **$173**

D **Farm jeep and trailer.** How pleased your little boy will be when he gets this farm jeep set! His "pretend" farm will be really up-to-date. Jeep is copied from an army jeep; substantially constructed of sturdy molded composition, with attractive bright enamel finish. Trailer is made of wood with composition wheels. Composition farmer has colorful painted-on clothes. Overall size, about 3¾x3⅜x12½ in. long.
49 N 5450—Shipping weight, 1 lb. 8 oz. .$1.39 **$139**

B **4-Piece Trailer Set.** This colorful, neatly designed, wooden trailer set makes a thrilling Christmas gift for any youngster who likes action. Hitch the four-wheeled hauler to the moving van with its door that opens into actual storage space, or attach it to the oil tanker or the open trailer. Each has sturdy black wheels and self-support at front. Hauler is 4½x 3½x2⅝ inches high. Trailers average about 7½ inches in length. Wooden hitches on front of each trailer.
49 N 5475—Shpg. wt., 2 lbs. 4 oz. . . . .Set $1.89 **$189**

E **Friendly walking doggie.** Doggie actually waggles along like a real puppy on a leash as tot pulls string. Imagine the thrill kiddies will get by owning a toy so full of action. They'll spend hours pulling the dog along, fascinated by the realistic motion of his legs. He's painted a life-like black and white, and his eyes have an appealing expression that's sure to endear him to everyone. Made of strong molded composition. Size, 11x7½x4 in.
49 N 5436—Shipping weight, 1 lb. 8 oz. .$1.29 **$129**

C **Realistic Farm Tractor.** Give this model tractor to that youngster you're especially fond of . . . if he loves playing "farmer", he'll be delighted to make such an important addition to his "farm". More than a toy for it produces a sound just like the motor of a real tractor. Red molded composition, black engine details. Swivel front wheels; trailer hitch in back. Rear wheels resemble balloon-type tires. A skillfully designed toy. Pull cord attached. Size of tractor, 8¼x5⅜x7 inches.
49 N 5471—Shipping weight, 2 pounds. .$1.79 **$179**

F **Waddling Duck with moving eyes.** It's true . . . he really waddles when pulled along. Kiddies will adore the funny walk of his flat, web-like feet; they'll be enchanted by the saucy glances from his gleaming black eyes. Made of strong composition, molded to resemble a real duck. Beautifully finished with colorful details that appeal to children. Sturdy pull cord attached size: 8x5x8½ inches high.
49 N 5437—Shipping weight, 1 lb. 8 oz. .$1.29 **$129**

It's easy to buy toys for your youngsters on Sears Easy Payment plan . . . see page 182C

PCB *SEARS-ROEBUCK . . PAGE 27*

1945 Sears catalog

Courtesy Tom Bishop

1946 Jim Brown catalog

Courtesy Tom Bishop

1946 Jim Brown catalog

Courtesy Tom Bishop

Whirling Blocks

An Action Toy to Thrill Your Child
Sturdily Built for Hard Use
All the Colors of the Rainbow

$1.49

A fine durable toy that will hold your youngster's attention for many hours on end. Has six colorful, shiny plastic blocks with large numerals and letters. Blocks whirl around as the little cart is pulled across the floor. Blocks fit on pegs in the composition platform and can be removed and used for building—or regular play. No rough or sharp edges to cut the hands or mouth—colors are harmless. Plastic wheels roll easily and cause the blocks to whirl. To clean blocks just wipe with a damp cloth. 9-inches long. Complete with cord.

No. 14M7501—Shpg. wt. 1 lb. Each...... **$1.49**

BIG SAVINGS IN PULL TOYS FOR CHILDREN

(A) Large Walking Duck   89c

A large sized life-like reproduction of a real duck. Actually walks with a shuffling rolling motion that is characteristic of a farmyard duck. Children find it is particularly amusing and will take it with them wherever they go.

Has large webbed feet and big sparkling eyes. Sturdy, full molded construction by NOMA the world famous toy makers. Body is finished in bright colors. Size: 9½-inches long, 4¾-inches wide and 8½-inches high. Pull cord and button included. Be sure to place your order early so the children will not be disappointed on Christmas morning.

No. 14M8808—Shpg. wt. 1 lb. 8 oz................ **89c**

(B) Action Steam Shovel $1.10

A dandy wooden toy that will keep idle hands busy—just the thing for a young son. The large size covered operators cab revolves like on a real steam shovel. The hand crank with oversize self locking handle will raise, lower and lock the scoop bucket in any position desired. The wide scoop bucket will actually pick-up articles and dispose of them where the young operator wishes. Tractor-type treads turn so steam shovel may be pulled into position. Carefully finished in bright, attractive colors. Size: 10¼-inches long and 9½-inches wide. Well made to withstand hard usage.

No. 14M8811—Shpg. wt. 2 lbs............. **$1.10**

(C) 3-Car Wooden Train Set   89c

A perfect gift at a low price. Especially fine for little tots 1 to 3 years of age. They'll shout with glee as they romp about the floor playing engineer. Set consists of a locomotive with coal tender, gondola for carrying blocks, marbles, etc., and a caboose with tiny windows. Each car is connected with easy-to-fasten pieces that make cars interchangeable. Sturdy wood construction for rough and tumble use. Wheels are free-running. All corners and edges are rounded. Painted in gay, attractive colors. Overall size is 30 inches long and 3 inches wide. Pull string and button included.

No. 14M8810—Shpg. wt. 2 lbs. Set................ **89c**

(D) Farm Tractor with Driver   98c

Boy! Just think of the fun your little boy will have with this large size heavy duty tractor. It looks just like the real thing with deep tread rear drive wheels and streamlined radiator. Makes a loud motor noise too, as it is pulled or pushed across the floor. Sturdily constructed to take hard wear. Large driving wheels have strong steel axle. Gayly painted farmer sits at steering wheel. Tractor is finished in bright red and black colors. Overall size: 8½ inches long and 5 inches wide. A real Christmas bargain at my low price.

No. 14M8809—Shpg. wt. 2 lbs. Each............. **98c**

(E) Clever Walking Dog   89c

Here is one of the cleverest, most popular children's toys ever put on the market. Every child that receives one this Christmas will get many hours of pleasure from him. The patented construction enables him to actually walk along like a real live dog when gently pulled across the floor. His large life-like body is 11-inches long, 7½-inches high and 4-inches wide. Made of durable wood composition and realistically painted white with large black spots. His long ears and mischievous looking face will endear him to your child. Pull cord attached.

Priced low to save you money at Christmastime—place your order early.

No. 14M8807—Shpg. wt. 1 lb. Each................. **89c**

(F) Farm Jeep and Trailer   69c

A fine low priced Christmas toy that will please any child from 1 to 8 years of age. Can be pulled by attached cord or pushed by hand. It's an accurate reproduction of the famous U. S. Army "Jeep" and includes a trailer for carrying blocks, small toys or other play articles. Jeep and farmer are made of durable, new Duro-Plastic. Jeep is 7-inches long, trailer wagon is of fine finished wood and is 5-inches long and 3-inches wide. Farmer is hand painted. All wheels and spare tire are plastic—cleverly designed even to the tire tread detail. Finished in attractive colors. Be sure to include this Jeep-Trailer on your Christmas order—it will help keep your youngster active and occupied.

No. 14M7582—Shpg. wt. 1-lb. 8-oz. Set............ **69c**

(G) Plastic Bulldozer and Farmer   54c

A long remembered present that your boy can play with in the sand box, back yard or living room floor—all year 'round. This big, husky bulldozer will make a fine companion machine for my farm tractor (D). It is made of thick, heavy plastic for hard, rugged use. While in motion, a special noise making ratchet makes this life-like caterpillar-type bulldozer sound like real. Operates on an off center roller that gives a wobbling motion. The pusher can be raised or lowered to follow the ground level. Has separate exhaust stack and a rear hook for attaching other rolling toys. Painted in bright colors of red and green. Farmer is hand painted. Overall length, including pusher in position—9¼-inches. Shipped in a heavy cardboard box—ready for gift wrapping.

No. 14M7583—Shpg. wt. 1-lb. 6-oz. Each. **54c**

NOTE: All items in this catalog are shipped Parcel Post EXCEPT those marked "Express Only." Turn to Pages 3 and 4 for complete shipping information.

Page 60   JIM BROWN   THE BROWN FENCE & WIRE CO., CLEVELAND, OHIO.—MEMPHIS, TENN.

1946 Jim Brown catalog

Courtesy Tom Bishop